FUCKBUDDY

THE MYTH OF THE FUCKBUDDY

JOHN FAITHFUL HAMER

Likeville Books

Montréal, Québec

for my sons,
Tristan and Indie,
who taught me, as only children can,
that love isn't a liquid asset
that can be readily spent on strangers;
it's inextricably tied up in relationships
with specific people.

Contents

Part V. Living Happily Everafter

Foreword: Worldly Knowledge

At 15, I wanted to know the world; at 25, I wanted to change it; at 35, I wanted to own it; but now, at 45, I find that I want to know it again, in intimate detail, the way a mother knows her child and a wise old rabbi knows the Torah; the way farmers know the earth and pastors know their flock; the way the organist knows his music and a shopkeeper knows his shop; the way my mother knows her river and my wife knows her garden; the way Darwin knew his finches and Galileo knew the stars; the way a man in love knows the constellation of freckles on his lover's inner thigh, and knows it so well, that he can sketch it from memory, onto a napkin at Else's, when she's a thousand miles away.

Preface: Sex Ed

"We have to learn to love, learn to be charitable, and this from our youth up; if education and chance offer us no opportunity to practice these sensations our soul will grow dry and even incapable of understanding them in others."—Friedrich Nietzsche, "Learning to Love," *Human, All Too Human* (1878)

Montreal was in the middle of an HIV epidemic when I was a kid. AIDS was no longer an exclusively gay problem. What's more, teen pregnancy was on the rise in the province, and sexually transmitted infections like gonorrhea, syphilis, and chlamydiae were growing resistant to the antibiotics used to treat them. It was a public health disaster and the Quebec government treated it as such. They embarked upon a remarkably ambitious program of sexual education aimed, not at high schools, but at elementary schools. The idea was to get to the kids in Grade Five and Grade Six: well *before* they hit puberty, and well *before* they became sexually active.

My friends and I were in Grade Five when they implemented the new Sex Ed curriculum. The sixth graders got a cool young teacher from NDG, a sexually liberated extrovert who seemed to genuinely enjoy covering the material. We got Mr. Hogg, an uptight WASP who blushed through many of the first lessons. Poor guy. Those first couple of weeks must have been hell. We giggled incessantly like idiots, even after he politely asked us to stop, even after he threatened us with detention—indeed, even after he threatened us with suspension. Like shivering uncontrollably when you're running a high fever, there's something eerily involuntary about nervous laughter. I remember marveling at how utterly helpless I felt. We knew we were being disruptive, and we didn't want to waste another afternoon in detention, but we simply could not stop laughing.

If I was shocked at ten by what was included in the Sex Ed curriculum, I'm shocked at 45 by what's excluded. We learned that sex is risky, and we learned that sex has consequences; but they failed to mention that some of those risks and consequences are emotional. They taught us how to deal with a broken condom, but they didn't teach us how to deal with a broken heart. We learned a great deal about sex but practically nothing about love.

Introduction: Love's Fast-Forward Button

"I am neither virgin nor whore, and I choose to hold that space proudly, which is not easy to do. I've always felt pressured to be one or the other to suit some man's fantasy. But now, at 36, I can admit that, while I love to screw, I don't want to be degraded like a porn star, objectified like a whore . . . . And at 36 I can also admit that I can't do casual sex. If I sleep with someone, I start feeling an emotional bond, even though some sex workers and sex writers tell me that attachment is a myth propagated by the patriarchy to keep me sexually disempowered. It doesn't matter—I can't do it. Maybe that makes me uncool, unhip and undesirable, but I just don't care anymore."—Tracy Chabala, "The Orgy Prude: How I Finally Admitted I Don't Like Meaningless Porn-Star Sex," *Salon* (March 23, 2015)

Sex is love's fast-forward button. If you're normal, sooner or later, you're going to fall in love with the person you're sleeping with, or they're going to fall in love with you, whether you like it or not. "Passionate love," as Jonathan Haidt rightly observes in *The Happiness Hypothesis* (2006), "is a drug. Its symptoms overlap with those of heroin . . . and cocaine . . . . Passionate love alters the activity of several parts of the brain, including parts that are involved in the release of dopamine. Any experience that feels intensely good releases dopamine, and the dopamine link is crucial here because drugs that artificially raise dopamine levels, as do heroin and cocaine, put you at risk of addiction."[1]

My guess is that it takes, on average, about a year for genuine intimacy and closeness to develop between new friends, unless the two of you share some sort of extreme experience (e.g., getting kidnapped together at gun-point by terrorists, getting trapped in an elevator for hours during an earthquake, fighting side-by-side in the trenches of a faraway war, talking on ecstasy for ten hours straight at a Baltimore rave, etc.). But if you're sleeping with the same person, you can attain the same level of intimacy in less than two weeks.

The feelings we develop for someone we're sleeping with are real and powerful and intense, as is the attachment, the craving, and the newfound neediness. This is largely a function of oxytocin, a hormone normally associated with mother-infant bonding in the animal kingdom. In most mammals, oxytocin is released solely during breastfeeding, where it helps to forge a powerful bond between mother and child. But in certain species, such as our own, large quantities of oxytocin are also released during sex, where it helps to forge a powerful bond between lovers. In *Blueprint* (2019), Nicholas A. Christakis maintains that these modifications of the oxytocin reflex are nothing short of astounding: "a set of physiological experiences that originally evolved to facilitate mother-child bonding" have, in *Homo sapiens*, evolved to facilitate and support pair-bonding. "The neural circuits that light up in a woman's brain are similar whether she looks at her baby or her partner."[2]

There's strength in numbers but peace in solitude. Hence the paradox of social life Freud ably described in *Civilization and Its Discontents* (1930): we need the strength in numbers that comes with

1. Jonathan Haidt, *The Happiness Hypothesis* (2006).
2. Nicholas A. Christakis, *Blueprint: The Evolutionary Origins of a Good Society* (2019).

social life, but, at one and the same time, social life makes demands upon us that often make us miserable.

A species composed of rugged individualists who really didn't need each other would have gone extinct long ago. We're not particularly strong or fast. Like bees and ants, our strength is derived primarily from our preternatural ability to work together. But why bother when people can be so annoying? Because we need them. Indeed, evolution seems to have selected for human neediness. Among other things, this explains the voracious nature of human sexuality. Unlike tigers, bears, and salamanders, who only have sex during the mating season, human beings have sex all year round. What's more, we have a great deal of sex that's clearly not going to result in pregnancy (e.g., gay sex, straight sex after menopause, etc.). This suggests that sex's primary purpose has long since transcended procreation.

Sexual desire renders us needy. It takes us out of ourselves and into the world, making hunters of us all. If the greatest friendships fall into our laps serendipitously, like the treasure you find buried in your own backyard, the greatest loves of our lives are like spoils we bring home from the field of battle.

PART I

THE WISDOM OF INNOCENCE

Thus speaks the man in love: autárkeia, self-sufficiency, the philosopher's ideal, has exited stage left—along with my Libran keel. Take my free will, for I wish to be your predestined fool. Slavery to you, my dear, shall henceforth for me be the rule. I cannot feign nonchalance, or Castiglione cool. A knowing look from your gentle eyes, and I am intoxicated with the strength of Samson, but a trivial slight from those very same green tyrants shears me of my former boldness and puts my stomach in knots. Oh Epictetus, wipe that disapproving look off your face! Stern Stoic, surrender to Aphrodite, and join the human race. You thought the poets hedonists and simpletons. But they saw something, something you and Buddha missed: a losing game it is, fleeing from fear and desire, for if you win, what have you won?

1.

Lake Lovering

"In truth, your beloved is just another human being, no different in essence from the multitudes you ignore every day on the train and in the supermarket. But to you, he or she seems infinite, and you are happy to lose yourself in that infinity. . . . If you are really in love with someone, you never worry about the meaning of life. And what if you are not in love? Well, if you believe in the romantic story but you are not in love, you at least know what the aim of your life is: to find true love."—Yuval Noah Harari, *21 Lessons for the 21st Century* (2018)

It was the summer of 1990, I was fifteen, and I was in love. We'd been together for about a year. Our friend Kay hatched an ingenious plan, the teenage equivalent of a Ponzi scheme really. Everybody told their parents that they were going to a friend's cottage (TRUE). Everybody said parents would be there (FALSE). The Arthur Andersen worthy ways in which we pulled off this scam would have made the smartest guys in the room at Enron beam with pride. But I'll spare you the details. Suffice it to say that ten of us, all underage, piled into a rickety old van and made our way down to a cottage on Lake Lovering, an hour and a half south of Montreal, where we'd be alone for four days (FOUR DAYS!) without *any* adult supervision.

Of course what followed was a comedy of errors. First we got lost.

A trip that should have taken an hour and a half took almost six hours. Then we ran out of gas just as we pulled into the driveway. Turns out, one of those flashing lights was the gas light. We arrived at the cottage a little before midnight. Exhausted. Hungry. Pissed Off. Badly in need of a good night's sleep. But that would not come, not for awhile, because of the fleas.

Kay's mom's best friend had, we later on discovered, stayed at the cottage the previous weekend with her three, big, flea-infested dogs. She and her dogs had, at some point, gone back to Montreal. But most of the fleas stayed. And they were starving. The fleas started biting soon after we walked into the cottage with our bags and gear. Most of us were bleeding and crazed before long. Took us an hour to find some Raid. Another hour or two to kill them all. That first night was terrible. Didn't get to sleep until three or four in the morning.

The following morning we realized that we hadn't brought nearly enough food. We realized, as well, that we'd forgotten to pick up some beer (a shocking oversight, all things considered). Had to get gas too. We knew we were going to have to walk into town. But Kay assured us that it wasn't far. Maybe an hour. Turns out, it was more like two. It was an altogether gendered division of labor: the girls stayed at the cottage to clean up whilst the guys trekked into town to get supplies. Took us about two hours to get there and—since we were now heavy-laden with food, gas, and cases of two-four—about three hours to get back.

The girls had gone wild while we were gone. First they helped themselves to Kay's mom's private stash of wine coolers. Then they decided to go skinny dipping in Lake Lovering. We arrived, shirtless and sweaty, upon a scene straight out of Homer. It was paradise: laughing mermaids frolicking in the midday sun. My girlfriend and I did it later on that day. It was her first time. My first time too. And we were so in love. So in love on Lake Lovering.

But then everything went to shit. Our parents found out where we were (somehow). On Sunday, a posse of pissed-off parental lawmakers piled into a Pontiac, got on the highway, and made their way south: to bring justice to the Eastern Townships. We didn't see them coming. Didn't hear them coming either. Because we were blasting our music. Because we were wasted. Because we were dancing around outside, frolicking in the sunshine half-naked in a place outside of time, a place that felt like heaven.

The parents arrived, fuming and furious, upon a decadent scene straight out of Bosch's *Garden of Earthly Delights*. They quickly transformed it into a dreadful scene straight out of Dante's *Inferno*. I remember thinking: this is it: this is *the* worst moment of my life. But it wasn't. Not even close. The bad memories faded long ago. All I remember now is the play of the sun on the water, the laughter of the mermaids, and the smell of my girlfriend's perfume. It was beautiful: Estée Lauder's Beautiful.

2.

The Wisdom of Innocence

It's one of social science's greatest hits: a fidgety little kid sits alone, in a room, with a marshmallow. He can eat it now if he wants. Won't get in trouble for doing so. But if he can refrain from eating it for fifteen minutes, he'll get another one when the grownup comes back. The film footage is laugh outloud funny. Some of the kids cave right away. Some try to cheat the system by taking little nibbles. And some hold out heroically for five or ten agonizing minutes before snatching up the precious like Gollum. But some of them go the distance.

When researchers checked in on these kids two decades later, some interesting patterns emerged. The kids who caved right away were far more likely to be drug addicts, high school dropouts, teen parents, criminals, overweight, depressed—whilst those who went the distance were far more likely to stay out of trouble and do well in school. These little gold-star bespeckled overachievers had something from an early age, something their prodigal peers lacked: namely, willpower (the ability to delay gratification). And this was key to their success. Or so we thought.

Turns out, kids who go the distance aren't blessed with extraordinary willpower; they're blessed with extraordinary parents. They're willing to wait for the second marshmallow because they trust that the grownup who made the promise is going to keep his word. They trust the grownup because they've grown up in loving homes, surrounded by grownups who keep their word—stable, predictable grownups—grownups you can trust. These kids trust the adult world because it's proven trustworthy. They're privileged. And their privilege has made them naïve. But there's a wisdom in this naïveté, just as there's a wisdom in innocence.

We're often told in this day and age that the privileged are all deluded and the underprivileged see things as they are. In practice, this is usually just a covert defense of the cynical perspective, because seeing things clearly always seems to mean seeing things cynically. Regardless, I don't buy it. Never have. I think lack of privilege reveals just as much as it conceals. Just as you need to have seen blue things to understand what blue is, you need to have experienced beauty and love and order to know what beauty and love and order are.

If you've never met a trustworthy grownup, you might be tempted to conclude that trustworthy grownups don't exist. If you've never experienced true love, you might be tempted to conclude that it's a myth. And if you've never seen government work well, you might be tempted to conclude that good government is a myth. You have to believe that "Another World is Possible" before you can make another world possible.

3.

Colorblindness and Cynicism

We often imagine that people who are exceptionally good at something are endowed with special strengths, extraordinary talents, or rare virtues. However, as Nassim Nicholas Taleb quite rightly maintains, this isn't always or even usually the case: "Success in all endeavors requires the absence of specific qualities: 1) To succeed in crime requires absence of empathy. 2) To succeed in banking you need absence of shame at hiding risks. 3) To succeed in school requires absence of common sense."

Success is often a function of some sort of absence. Seeing through camouflage is a case in point. We now know that there's an upside to colorblindness: the colorblind can see through many kinds of camouflage. Because they're not distracted by colors, they can often see the contours of a thing—its outline—with unusual clarity. Even so, despite this upside, being colorblind is, on balance, a net handicap to the colorblind individual. They're missing out on a great deal.

I've always been amazed by people like my friend Aaron Haspel: people who know how to cut through the crap with ease; people with extremely well developed bullshit meters; people who are exceptionally good at discerning the real motives behind actions; people who always seem to know what's really going on; people, in short, who are exceptionally cynical. But I've long since noticed that these very same people frequently fail to see a great deal that the rest of us mere mortals do see.

Cynics often sneeringly maintain that whatever they can't see or experience isn't real (e.g., true love, genuine altruism, empathy, divinity, spirituality, transcendence, communion with nature, etc.). And this leads me to suspect that those who are especially good at seeing through bullshit pay dearly for their gift. I suspect that being able to see past nuance comes at a cost. The ability to rapidly reduce complicated moral questions into simple either/or propositions is probably a function of an absence. The moral clarity of most cynics is probably a function of some sort of emotional colorblindness.

Learning about humanity from the cynical is like learning about wildlife from roadkill.

4.

Question Everything

"Ana Montes wasn't a master spy. She didn't need to be. In a world in which our lie detector is set to the off position, a spy is always going to have an easy time of it."—Malcolm Gladwell, *Talking to Strangers: What We Should Know About the People We Don't Know* (2019)

A few years ago I was asked to buy a t-shirt. It was part of a fundraiser for a local philosophy department's student association. The slogan blazoned across the chest read: QUESTION EVERYTHING. It made me smile, the way that cheesy Hallmark cards often make me smile.

We simply don't have the time or energy to question everything. We all rely upon people and things we don't understand. We trust the people on the highway not to veer into oncoming traffic. We trust that the food we're eating isn't poisoned. We trust that the people we leave our children with aren't going to hurt them. We trust that the money we use has real value. We trust that the people who say they love us actually love us, despite the fact that we can never really be sure. We can never really know another person's heart, not with certainty. And so on and so forth. We are swimming in a sea of trust each and every day.

People who've had their faith in the world profoundly shaken by a psychotic break, a horrible accident, or a devastating betrayal—people who *actually* question everything—are broken, profoundly dysfunctional shells of their former selves. At Projet PAL in Verdun, I worked with people who were recovering from severe mental health problems. What's hardest for many of these people is that they feel like they can no longer trust their own senses. They're tormented by questions such as: Am I *really* talking to you? Are you *really* real? Is this *really* how I feel? Can I trust my feelings?

The same is true of those who've lived through a devastating betrayal. We've all known people who've been cheated on and habitually lied to. But imagine what it must be like to be Paula Rader, the woman who discovered that the man she was married to for 34 years, Dennis Rader, the father of her children, was the notorious serial killer known as the BTK killer. She thought her husband was a good man. They went to Christ Lutheran every Sunday morning. He was even elected president of the church council.

How hard it must be for Paula Rader to trust people now. How hard it must be for her to trust her own judgment. She must be tormented by questions such as: How could I have been so stupid? So blind? Hard as it must be, the Paula Raders of this world won't be able to resume anything like a normal life until they begin to trust again, until they learn how to have faith again. Because faith isn't a choice. It's a necessity.

5.

Romantic Interlude I: Intellectual Fashion Victim

"Relationships are exquisitely sensitive to balance in their early stages, and a great way to ruin things is either to give too much (you seem perhaps a bit desperate) or too little (you seem cold and rejecting). Rather, relationships grow best by balanced give and take, especially of gifts, favors, attention, and self-disclosure."—Jonathan Haidt, *The Happiness Hypothesis* (2006)

I was all bent of shape. Or so says the diary. It was January 12, 2000. My new girlfriend Anna-Liisa and I had recently consolidated our book collections (that is, moved-in together). I was perusing her sweet contributions to the stacks when I stumbled upon an inscription she'd written to an ex-boyfriend. (Incidentally, the douche had returned the book after the breakup: a clear violation of breakup etiquette: keep or destroy, never return). Regardless, in her eloquent, paragraph-long inscription, she employed a beautiful turn of phrase which she'd once used in an early love letter to me! I was mortified! Heartbroken! Pissed! Felt like I'd been dealt a shabby hand of recycled Valentine's Day sentiments. Felt like I'd been played.

But that wore off pretty quick. Outrage soon gave way to embarrassment, and I started to feel pretty stupid. She is who she is, I reasoned, and this turn of phrase is, at bottom, as much a part of her as her accent. It's unreasonable of me to expect her to reinvent herself every time she gets into a new relationship. How could I have possibly come to see that as a reasonable expectation? How could I possibly be so lame? She can recycle good material as much as she wants to, I concluded, so long as she uses her lines on one dude at a time.

That's when I realized, much to my chagrin, that I was a fashion victim, an intellectual fashion victim, of two broad cultural currents: Late Capitalism, with its obsessive focus on intellectual property, and 1960s-era Romanticism, with its obsessive focus on authenticity and originality. When I discovered my new girlfriend's inscription in an ex-boyfriend's ex-book, two turbulent tributaries—capitalism and romanticism—emptied themselves into the river of my mind, creating much white water, a fishy smell, and a will-o'-the-wisp that terrified me for a moment or two, until I saw him for what he was.

PART II

THE BATTLE OF THE SEXES IS BULLSHIT

I watched a grown woman teach her boyfriend how to ride a bike today. They were in their thirties. It may be the most beautiful thing I'll see this month. The two of them giggling incessantly, very much in love, his wobbly wheels crunching through the autumn leaves.

6.

World's Worst Girlfriend

"There is only one person to whom we can expose our catalog of grievances, one person who can be the recipient of all our accumulated rage at the injustices and imperfections of our lives. It is of course the height of absurdity to blame them. But this is to misunderstand the rules under which love operates. It is because we cannot scream at the forces who are really responsible that we get angry with those we are sure will best tolerate us for blaming them. We take it out on the very nicest, most sympathetic, most loyal people in the vicinity, the ones least likely to have harmed us, but the ones most likely to stick around while we pitilessly rant at them."—Alain de Botton, *The Course of Love* (2018)

It was a beautiful ceremony but a terrible reception. And I was stuck at the worst table in the room, sitting across from the worst couple in the world. A real match made in Hell. They were in the middle of some sort of fight. She was mad at him. Really mad. Furious actually. But he didn't know why. Poor guy kept sheepishly asking her what was wrong. Eventually she told him. Apparently she was mad at him because he'd said something horribly hurtful the night before. At dinner.

He stared at her with the doe eyes of an innocent man. He really didn't know what the fuck she was talking about. Seriously, if you looked up "WTF?" in the dictionary, there'd be a picture of this dude's face. Didn't last though. Second or two later, color in the dude's face went from Scared-Rabbit White to Righteously-Indignant Red. Faster than you can say Johnnie Cochran. Guy was so mad he was shaking. Could barely speak. He reminded her that he was on a plane last night. That they didn't talk last night. That he'd been back home for a funeral. His grandmother's funeral.

Took awhile, but eventually she realized that she wasn't remembering something that actually happened, something he actually said; she was remembering something he'd said to her last night in a dream. Did she apologize? Nope. She doubled down. Said the dream spoke to a deeper truth about their relationship even if it wasn't factually true.

7.

Pigeons and Peregrines

The pigeon pecking at the baguette keeps an eye on the peregrine perched nearby. The falcon, eating her meal, does so in peace, losing herself in the pleasure of the moment, like a wine-soaked Epicurean.

Isn't it always so? Parents have more illusions about their kids than their kids have about them. Employers have more illusions about their employees than their employees have about them. Masters have more illusions about their slaves than their slaves have about them. And men have more illusions about women than women have about men.

The powerful can afford to be self-absorbed. Those who lack power cannot: they must be watchful, vigilant, alert, and aware. They must observe the powerful carefully. So the slave comes to know her master—better, perhaps, than he knows himself—but the master can't remember her name.

*

The monster in Wes Craven's *A Nightmare on Elm Street* (1984), Freddy Krueger, kills his victims in their dreams. So long as you can stay awake, so long as you can refrain from sleeping, you're safe. But, as you might expect, the young people who Krueger stalks can only stay up for so long. Eventually they fall asleep. And when they do, as they all eventually do, he uses a glove armed with razors to slice his victims into pieces.

The monster in Emily Yoffe's *Slate* article on sexual assault "lurks where women drink like a lion at a watering hole."[1] Though mitigated with caveat after caveat, Yoffe's advice to young women is about as stupid as that given to the young people in *A Nightmare on Elm Street*. So long as you can stay sober, so long as you can refrain from drinking, you're safe. What's ironic is that Yoffe clearly views her advice as pragmatic. It is, in fact, quite idealistic. It's also unrealistic.

Drinking has been a central part of youth culture for thousands of years. There are plenty of good and bad reasons for this. But that's another conversation for another day. What matters here is that we pragmatically acknowledge one simple fact: partying is a central feature of college life, and that's unlikely to change anytime soon. As such, asking young women to avoid it—for their own good—is profoundly unfair. Why should they have to miss out on a big part of the college experience? Is it any wonder that they ignore us? I would.

The nightmare on Elm Street is caused by Freddy Krueger. He's the problem. Not the young people who keep falling asleep. Likewise, the nightmare on College Street is caused by sexual predators like Brock Turner, the Stanford swimmer who sexually assaulted an unconscious woman behind a dumpster on January 17th, 2015. They're the problem. Not the young women who keep drinking.

I partied like a champ back in the day, as did most of my friends, and it did lead to some stupid decisions. It occurred to some of us to take on a bouncer twice our size. Or a football player three times our size. Fair amount of fighting happened. But it just didn't occur to any of us to rape. And we were regularly around passed out drunk girls.

1. Emily Yoffe, "College Women: Stop Getting Drunk," *Slate* (October 15, 2013).

That's why I just don't buy this whole "WHOOPS, I RAPED HER" defense.

There are plenty of things that guys who are "totally out of control" refrain from doing almost all the time (e.g., stabbing pets to death, stealing from friends, sticking forks into electrical outlets, cutting their own dicks off for fun, etc.). If drunk guys were just as likely to rape as they were to cut off their own limbs, or jump out of penthouse windows, I'd be prepared to take the diminished capacity argument seriously. But we all know that's simply not the case.

If drunk words are sober thoughts, drunk actions are sober fantasies. And full-blown fantasies aren't born full-grown. To rape when you're drunk, you've gotta be fantasizing about it a whole lot when you're sober. And what kind of a culture produces a steady supply of kids who fantasize about raping each other?

There have always been a small number of weirdos and outliers with strange desires (e.g., cannibals, necrophiliacs, bestialitists). These people are rare events, black swans, freaks of nature. The parents who produce them, and the communities who nurture them, can't be held responsible for their fantasies. Nor can they be held responsible for their actions. The same cannot be said of the Brock Turners of this world. Because their fantasies are anything but rare. And their crimes are all too common.

There are people in our midst who think it's totally appropriate to use someone else's body like a blowup doll with a pulse. If we're ever to wake up from this nightmare on College Street, *your* tragedy must cease to be *their* fantasy.

*

We now know that Hindus used to eat beef. Cows weren't always sacred to them. And eating them wasn't always prohibited. Historians of Ancient India believe that the prohibition against eating beef spread slowly at first, over the course of decades, maybe even centuries; but after reaching some sort of tipping point, this quirky regional taboo became a rigid subcontinental norm. And it did so with remarkable speed: one year your neighbors are gossiping about you because you eat beef, giving you dirty looks; next year they're burning your house to the ground for doing so, driving you out of town.

The India that emerged out of this massive cultural shift was, in essence, a safe space for cows. Unattended cows can walk down streets and alleyways lined with the hungry in India, and they can do so fearlessly, nonchalantly, without a care in the world. They can do so because the taboo boundaries against harming them are well-established, well-guarded, and rigidly enforced.

Are we living through a cultural shift of a similar stamp? It certainly looks like it. After decades of disappointment, we appear to have reached some sort of a feminist tipping point in the civilized West. Sexist behavior that was merely considered uncouth a generation ago is now deemed thoroughly disgusting and decidedly uncool; men who were merely seen as pigs back in the day have been redefined, seemingly overnight, as criminals and degenerates.

The society that emerges from this messy cultural shift has yet to take shape. But this much is clear: it will be a safer space for women and children. It will be safer because the taboo boundaries against harming them will be well-established, well-guarded, and rigidly enforced. Who knows, we may soon find ourselves living in a brave new world, a radically transformed moral landscape, wherein women and children can walk down streets and alleyways fearlessly, nonchalantly, without a care in the world.

Isaiah dreamed of a peaceful world without predation: "The wolf shall dwell with the lamb, and the leopard shall lie down with the young goat . . . and the lion shall eat straw like the ox."[2] John Lennon dreamed of a peaceful world without religion, nation states, and private property: "Imagine no possessions / I wonder if you can / No need for greed or hunger / A brotherhood of man / Imagine all the people / Sharing all the world."[3] Are we dreaming dreams of a similar stamp? Maybe this what it feels like when somebody presses history's fast-forward button.

*

Between the ages of twelve and fourteen, when I was at my most awkward, I worked as a bagger at a grocery store: Steinberg's in Alexis-Nihon Plaza. There was this cashier that me and the other lowly baggers looked up to. He was a good looking guy in his early twenties. I swear he must have slept with half of Montreal. I've never met a better pickup artist. He could get half a dozen phone numbers on a Saturday afternoon. While he was working! It was insane. And he made it look easy. We called him the Steinberg Stud.

I remember hanging on his every word in the break room, with the other zitty dorks, as he revealed the masculine mysteries to us in hushed tones. He referred to his seduction technique as "The Scratch Ticket Strategy": "If you wanna win the lottery, what do you do? You buy a lot of lottery tickets, right? It's really that simple, guys. Just keeping buying them until you get a winner. Same is true of tail. If you wanna get a lot of ass, you've gotta hit on everything that moves. You've gotta be shameless."

Unlike Tucker Max, author of *Assholes Finish First* (2010), the Steinberg Stud wasn't trying to trick women into sleeping with him. He wasn't a misogynistic asshole either. He was just an extremely friendly guy who put himself out there again and again and again. So far as I could tell, women liked him because he was (a) really

2. Isaiah 11:6.
3. John Lennon, *Imagine* (1971).

good looking, (b) extremely charming, and (c) genuinely interested in them.

As Nassim Nicholas Taleb makes clear in *Antifragile* (2012), people who are successful at something are often blissfully unaware of *why* they're successful at it. They might *think* they know why they're successful, but they're often dead wrong. He refers to this as the "green lumber fallacy", after a trader who made a fortune buying and selling green lumber without knowing what it was. He thought green lumber was actually green as opposed to freshly cut.

The reigning king of the pickup artists, Daryush Valizadeh (Roosh V), has obviously fallen prey to the green lumber fallacy. What a profoundly delusional idiot this guy is! He actually thinks that his sociopathic skills are what gets him laid. Of course it's obvious to any objective outside observer with common sense—indeed, even to hard-core feminists like Laurie Penny, who loathe him—that he gets laid a lot because he's hot: "Roosh is tall and well-built and actually rather good-looking for, you know, a monster."[4]

Of all the sad specimens I meet in this broken and burning world, few evoke more spontaneous sympathy than straight guys who seem to be prisoners of their own sexuality. Some of these guys, like Roosh V, are downright misogynists; but, in my experience, most are not. Women are simply a mystery to them, a mystery they're not interested in solving. Gender is for them a kind of tall garden wall, a barrier made of solid stone, which keeps them from seeing women as people. These guys are happiest when they're hanging out with the guys. It's now common to speak of gender dysphoria (e.g., being a woman trapped in a man's body). Perhaps we need to start talking about an equally tragic condition: sexuality dysphoria.

---

4. Laurie Penny, "I'm With The Banned," *Medium* (July 21, 2016).

8.

Laughing at Louis CK

Louis CK's comedy appeals to diverse groups of people precisely because it's complex. Everyone in the room is laughing, but they're laughing for profoundly different reasons. I realized this for the first time after watching *Live at the Beacon Theater* (2011) with a room full of friends. Some were laughing at him, and some were laughing with him. Still others believed that they were in the presence of a modern-day Diogenes, a radically honest man who tells the unvarnished truth, come what will. It's this last group that worries me—not, I hasten to add, because there's anything wrong with telling the truth, but because there's something wrong with thinking that your truth is The Truth.

We all have a tendency to believe that our experience is somehow universal. This is a human, all-too-human tendency. That said, people with a great deal of privilege—people like me (i.e., white men of a certain class)—seem to get a double-portion of this tendency. Louis CK's comedy is a case in point. Part of what makes it so effective is a complicated cocktail of awareness to privilege and blindness to privilege. He sees his own privilege with astounding accuracy, and yet, at one and the same time, he speaks about his inner life with a naïve presumptuousness which is, in and of itself, a hallmark of privilege.

The assumption behind much of Louis CK's comedy—sometimes stated, sometimes implied—is that his own experience is normative. His message to men is more or less as follows: Come on guys, we're among friends now, quit the bullshit. The chicks aren't listening now, so stop trying to be politically correct. You know, and I know, that you're feeling and thinking and doing exactly the same things I'm thinking and feeling and doing.

Eddie Murphy's stand-up comedy has always relied heavily upon this technique. For instance, in *Raw* (1987), he asks all of the men in the audience "that are loyal to their women" to clap. Though it seems like a perfectly innocent question, we soon realize that it was posed in bad faith. A moment or two after the crowd bursts into applause, Murphy interrupts them loudly, shouting: "Stop! You lying motherfuckers, stop. Stop, stop, stop. Kiss my ass. Fuck, there ain't no such thing as a loyal man, you lying motherfuckers. Stop it. Yeah, the only reason you're clapping is because your woman's sitting next to you right now when I asked you. . . . Get the fuck out. . . . All men fuck other women. We are low by nature and have to do it. . . . All men do it. We have to do it. . . . It is a man thing. . . . It is a dick thing. Do not try to understand it. You have to have a dick to understand this."

Were some of the men in Eddie Murphy's audience lying? Sure. Were all of them lying? I highly doubt it. Be that as it may, what's key to note here is that Murphy categorically refuses to entertain some entirely plausible possibilities, such as the existence of loyal men, and the existence of women who truly get men ("You have to have a dick to understand this."). It's also interesting to note that Murphy is making some pretty categorical claims about what it means to be a man ("All men do it. We have to do it. . . . It is a man thing."). Regardless, I call bullshit.

I know plenty of guys who don't fit into Murphy's straitjacket, just as I know plenty of guys who don't fit into Louis CK's straitjacket.

THE MYTH OF THE FUCKBUDDY

I know plenty of guys who love fatherhood and find married life delightful. Sure, they have bad days, even bad weeks—but, on balance, they really enjoy the life of the householder. What's more, I know plenty of grown men who aren't tormented—as Louis CK and Eddie Murphy seem to be—by a never-ending torrent of pornographic thoughts. I know plenty of grown men who really don't picture every woman they know naked, who really don't fantasize about fucking every woman they know.

Are these guys an unrepresentative sample of Dude Nation? Perhaps. But I doubt it. Because I've got male friends from all walks of life: from the ultra-conservative to the ultra-liberal. Are these guys lying to me? Perhaps. But I doubt it. Because I'm always sure to bring up these sorts of questions in the wee hours of the morning, at the end of a long night, when we're all fairly drunk (or high), speaking in confidence among friends, and inclined towards the kind of brutal honesty that makes these conversations so memorable. These guys aren't laughing with Louis CK; they're laughing at him. The great genius of Louis CK is that he shows us how much of a living hell it must be to be a teenage boy stuck in a grown man's life.

*

Don Lorenzetti, my childhood karate teacher, my sensei, loomed large in the working-class Verdun of my youth. This is due, in part, to the extreme scarcity of worthwhile father figures in my neighborhood. At least a third of my friends lived, like me, in single-parent households where father was nowhere to be found; and at least half of those who did have fathers around, wished they didn't—because dad was a drunk, a lazy loser, a teenager trapped in a man's body, who smacked mom around from time to time, watched TV all day, and spent the rent.[1]

Don was the very opposite of this. He was a man who kept his

1. An earlier version of this section appeared in *The Post Millennial* (March 28, 2019).

promises, a grown man you could count on, and an adult who always acted like an adult. In the midst of a thoroughly screwed-up neighborhood—wracked with record levels of unemployment, a pernicious culture of poverty, and all sorts of social problems—there was the Centre de Karaté Verdun: an island of order in the midst of a sea of urban chaos.

Many of us looked up to Don. And for good reason: he was a thoroughly honorable man: a real mensch. He was more than just our sensei: for many of us, he was a moral exemplar and a fountain of wisdom. Though I'm 45 now, I find that I can remember much of what he said to us with astonishing word-for-word accuracy.

One hot summer night, when we were all clowning around like idiots in the dojo, Don lost it and thundered: "The boy must die for the man to live!" We fell silent, froze, and blushed in unison. You could hear a pin drop. His words stung, not because we feared him, but because we loved him, respected him, and desperately wanted to please him. We wanted to kill the stupid boys within us. He made us want to be men.

Although I grew up in a single-parent household, I was able to find father figures (e.g., my uncles, my pastor, my sensei, a few teachers, a professor, etc.). And these guys made all the difference in my life. But this happened, in large part, because my single mom recognized the need for them and actively supported solutions. This went against the received progressive feminist wisdom of the time, which maintained that fathers, father figures, and indeed men in general, were completely unnecessary.

*

Those who maintain that gender roles are written in stone are at least as wrong as those who say that we're all more or less interchangeable. Our species has benefited from the diversity of groups and the flexibility of individuals. We are, at one and the same time, special snowflakes and social Swiss army knives. Like hockey players on a small town team, we evolved in small groups that couldn't afford to overspecialize: everybody (or nearly everybody) had to be able to play every position in a pinch (e.g., women needed to be able to hunt and fight, even if men were, on average, better at hunting and fighting; and men needed to be able to take care of children, even if women were, on average, better at taking care of children). Overspecialization is a luxury our ancestors could ill afford.

9.

The Battle of the Sexes is Bullshit

"In every instance of successful reconciliation save Mozambique justice was meted out, but never in full measure. This fact may be lamentable, even tragic, from certain legal or moral perspectives, yet it is consistent with the requisites of restoring social order postulated in the forgiveness hypothesis. In all cases of successful reconciliation, retributive justice could neither be ignored nor fully achieved. . . . Disturbing as it may be, people appear able to tolerate a substantial amount of injustice wrought by amnesty in the name of social peace."—William J. Long and Peter Brecke, *War and Reconciliation: Reason and Emotion in Conflict Resolution* (2003)

Just as there are plenty of good reasons to fight fair and refrain from cheating, there are plenty of good reasons to be graceful in victory and graceful in defeat. John McCain understood this far better than most. And he lived by it. As Lindsey Graham put it in his moving eulogy to McCain: "John taught us how to lose. When you go throughout the world, people remember his concession speech as much as anything else. There are so many countries where you can't afford to lose because they'll kill you." The peaceful transfer of power and gentle commerce are cornerstones of civilized life. Taking them for granted is decidedly unwise. Rejecting them outright is downright reckless (e.g., saying that if your side loses the election it'll be proof that the election was rigged, saying that anybody's who's got money stole it).

Ruthlessness is, for the most part, remarkably stupid and shortsighted. As every intelligent eight-year-old knows, getting invited to play the next game is the primary objective of every game. Winning is of secondary importance. If you'll do anything to win, you're not playing the game properly. War is an obvious exception to this rule. Ruthlessness is sometimes warranted when you're at war. Indeed, this is precisely why irresponsible culture warriors are always trying redefine peacetime activities in wartime terms through the use of martial vocabulary and military metaphors (e.g., "the war against women", "the war against boys", "the battle of the sexes", etc.).

In *Postwar* (2005), Tony Judt maintains that linguistic choices such as these were central to the way in which the Communist state justified its ruthlessness: "The Communist state was in a permanent condition of undeclared war against its own citizens. . . . The martial vocabulary so beloved of Communist rhetoric echoed this conflict-bound condition. Military metaphors abounded: class conflict required alliances, liaison with the masses, turning movements, frontal attacks."[1] Judt makes an important point here: namely, that there's something about the very language of Marxism that predisposes it towards violence. Susan Neiman makes the same point in a more fulsome fashion in *Evil in Modern Thought* (2002). This point is invariably overlooked by those who wish to exonerate Marx, vilify Lenin, and pretend that Stalin's horrific crimes are at best a perversion of the master's teachings. Slavoj Žižek, to his credit, is a notable exception to this mendacious rule. He forthrightly acknowledges the connection and affirms it, with a sangfroid I find rather disturbing.

---

1. Tony Judt, *Postwar: A History of Europe since 1945* (2005).

Regardless of your motivation, using martial language is profoundly irresponsible. As Lao Tzu rightly observed long ago, the language we use to describe present reality has a sneaky way of shaping future reality: "Watch your words, they become your actions; watch your actions, they become your habits; watch your habits, they become your character; watch your character, it becomes your destiny."[2] If you treat every competition like a life-or-death struggle, you'll soon find yourself in the middle of a life-or-death struggle. If you keep acting like you're at war, you'll eventually be at war. And if you keep treating me like the enemy, sooner or later, I'll be your enemy. Peacetime relations between political parties, regions, groups, and heterosexual partners are fundamentally corrupted by military metaphors. Language is a tool and these tools aren't the right ones for the job. Reaching for martial language when you're trying to make sense of run-of-the-mill marital problems is like reaching for a flame-thrower when you're trying to light a birthday cake.

At the dramatic climax of *Traffic* (2000), Michael Douglas's character, the guy in charge of the War on Drugs, breaks down in the middle of a press conference and goes off-script: "If there is a War on Drugs then our own families have become the enemy. How can you wage war on your own family?" The overarching message of Stephen Marche's *The Unmade Bed* (2018) is of a similar stamp: namely, that the martial language employed by culture warriors is a toxic dead-end. Men and women are not tribes locked in a zero-sum battle of the sexes. Your spouse is not the enemy: "The central conflict of domestic life right now is not mothers against fathers, or even conflicting ideas of motherhood or gender. It is the family against money." *The Unmade Bed* is a deeply moral book. And Marche treats his subject with all of the seriousness it deserves. But it's also a remarkably funny book. The following scene is a case in point: "I was at a bachelor party, one of those bizarre rituals in which men have to stoop to their stereotype as a kind of recognition of common

2. Lao Tzu, *Tao Te Ching* (1964). Translated by D. C. Lau.

brutality, and we were all drunkenly heading to a strip club when my wife called. She needed to talk. A man she worked with called her 'Honey.' It pissed her off. It pissed me off. It pissed me off that this classic old-school garbage should survive. And so I found myself enraged, genuinely enraged at the sexism of a world that would call my wife 'Honey' just as I was entering a business in which I was going to pay to see women naked. Such are the everyday minor anti-epiphanies of living through the twenty-first-century rearrangement of gender. They subtract from rather than add to what I thought I knew about myself and others." Marche's discussion of housework in the last chapter is equally hilarious: "Housework is the macho bullshit of women. And, in this light, it is perhaps not surprising that men have not started doing more housework. Men might be willing to lose the garbage of their own gender stereotypes, but why should they take on the garbage of another? Equality is coming, but not the way we expected. The future does not involve men doing more housework. . . . Caring less is the hope of the future. Housework is perhaps the only political problem in which doing less and not caring are the solution, where apathy is the most progressive and sensible attitude. Fifty years ago it was perfectly normal to iron sheets and vacuum drapes; they were necessary tasks. The solution to the inequalities of dusting wasn't dividing the dusting; it was not doing the dusting at all. The solution to the gender divide in housework generally is that simple: Don't bother. Leave the stairs untidy. . . . Never make the bed. . . . A clean house is the sign of a wasted life, truly. Eventually we'll all be living in perfect egalitarian squalor." As Marche demonstrates, in loving detail, we're all in this together whether we like it or not, and we're going to have to muddle through it together. We didn't create this mess, but it's ours to clean up: "Instead of furious despair, what our moment demands is humility and compassion."[3]

3. Stephen Marche, *The Unmade Bed: The Messy Truth about Men and Women in the 21st Century* (2018).

Life has always included a great deal of suffering, marriage has always been difficult, and our moment, like every moment in history, presents us with some unique challenges not faced by our forebears. But the twenty-first-century West is hardly the most challenging place and time to be alive. Much of the "furious despair" Marche speaks of is a function, not of especially difficult times, but of especially unrealistic expectations. We expect far too much of each other, and far too much of marriage; and these poorly calibrated expectations are making us miserable.

We need to become far better at distinguishing between problems and conditions. Problems have solutions, conditions do not. Conditions are merely managed to reduce the frequency and severity of symptoms. Some conditions turn out to be problems—problems with solutions (e.g., stomach ulcers). But the category error is more often made in the other direction. Many so-called problems are in fact conditions. For instance, most so-called "marital problems" are in fact marital conditions. As Jonathan Haidt put it the other day on the Likeville Podcast: "When you get married, you're basically choosing a set of unsolvable problems."[4]

Do you get into an epic fight about *x* at least once a month? Well, guess what, you'll probably be fighting about *x* twenty years from now. And that's fine. Make your peace with it. Quit searching for final solutions! Rather than trying to solve the problem of *x* once and for all, work on reducing the frequency and intensity of these fights: from, say, one horribly-upsetting-weekend-long emotional bloodbath to one twenty-minute-long spat every two or three months. As Epictetus rightly observed long ago, happiness and freedom are impossible without properly calibrated expectations such as these: "Happiness and freedom begin with a clear understanding of one principle: Some things are within our control, and some things are not. It is only after you have faced up to this

4. Jonathan Haidt, "The Happiness Hypothesis," *Likeville Podcast* E73 (December 2, 2019).

fundamental rule and learned to distinguish between what you can and can't control that inner tranquility and outer effectiveness become possible."[5]

Couples who've been together for a long time can fight so spectacularly because they're not just fighting about what happened today, yesterday, or last week; they're fighting about what happened last year, last decade, or even last century. As you might expect, this makes their fights far more intense than they ought to be. When this dynamic is ramped up to the group level, the results are depressingly predictable. First you get a whole lot of angry people screaming and yelling about stuff that happened centuries ago (to their ancestors) as if it happened yesterday (to them). Before long, a diabolical leader emerges, proposing violent reprisals, such as a program of ethnic cleansing.

Why don't we just forgive it all? What could be more beautiful than a periodic forgetting of debts? It could renew our relationships, our economy, our international relations? How often do we see people split up and remarry simply because the weight of resentment on their shoulders proves too heavy to bear? They start off fresh with a new partner, also recently divorced, and proceed, slowly but surely, to build up a similarly substantial weight of resentment—which will eventually necessitate yet another divorce, and yet another remarriage.

Why not break this cycle? Why not forgive the debts, get over it, stop bringing up old shit, and move on? Because we shouldn't ignore the claims of justice, you say. Because it's payback time. You want vengeance, reparations, public apologies, sackcloth and ashes. Very well, then, have at it, scale Mount Justice. Sometimes, alas, it's necessary. But be sure to count the cost. The air at the top of Mount

5. Epictetus, *The Art of Living: The Classical Manual on Virtue, Happiness, and Effectiveness* (2013). Translated by Sharon Lebell.

Justice is intoxicating, and the views are spectacular, but it's lonely up there.

10.

Romantic Interlude II: Single Lessons

"We learn what love is from movies and television, and it's ruined love for us. Romantic comedies, all that shit, it's ruined love. It's taught us that we are incomplete people who need to find that one person in the whole world that will complete us. I promise you, there are thousands of people that are perfectly good matches for any one of you. And I don't want to be completed. I'm working very hard to be a complete person every day, you know? I don't wanna make you whole. I want you to come whole. . . . And I know I just said 'cum hole.'"—Sarah Silverman, *Speck of Dust* (2017)

A friend of mine gave up on men in her mid-forties. She'd been in back-to-back relationships since she was thirteen. None of them good. So she threw in the towel. "Clearly I suck at this, John!" Of course she met the love of her life a few years later, and they've lived happily ever after since then. But before she met Mr. Right, she was single for a few years, truly single, for the first time in her life. She said it was enlightening, being single. She said she learned how to take responsibility for her own emotions: "Back in the day, if I woke up in a bad mood, I'd turn to the guy next to me and say: 'I feel bad because you did X or you didn't do Y.' But when I was single, if I woke up in a bad mood, there was no one to blame. I had to stop blaming others for my sadness. Making others responsible for my happiness."

If taking responsibility for your own emotions is like finishing Spiritual High School, what might we learn in Spiritual College? If Epictetus is to be believed, the next step is to get rid of the impulse to blame altogether: "Small-minded people habitually reproach others for their own misfortunes. Average people reproach themselves. Those who are dedicated to a life of wisdom understand that the impulse to blame something or someone is foolishness, that there is nothing to be gained in blaming, whether it be others or oneself. One of the signs of the dawning of moral progress is the gradual extinguishing of blame. We see the futility of finger-pointing."[1]

If getting over our obsession with finger-pointing is like finishing Spiritual College, what might we learn in Spiritual Grad School? If Kant is to be believed, the next step is to take responsibility for the happiness of others. Philosopher Susan Neiman summarizes his reasoning in *Moral Clarity* (2008): "Like most people, you're likely to devote most of your attention to your own happiness (or lack thereof), and my perfection (or lack thereof). What if we simply switched? Devote yourself to my happiness and your own perfection, and I'll do the same in return. In a world where everyone did *that*, both happiness and virtue would double."[2]

Learning to love yourself *isn't* the greatest love of all.

---

1. Epictetus, *The Art of Living* (2013).
2. Susan Neiman, *Moral Clarity: A Guide for Grown-Up Idealists* (2008).

PART III

SCRABBLE, ECSTASY, & FERTILITY CLINICS

If I was on the Titanic when it began to sink, I'm pretty sure I would have been one of those fools who polished the silverware and rearranged the furniture all the way down; or maybe I would have been one of those silly men sitting there at the ship's bar—sipping whiskey, talking too much, laughing out loud, totally oblivious—even as the iceberg tore chunks out of the mahogany wall, and ice-cold saltwater poured into the smoky pub.

If we're going to philosophize, it's going to involve walking or wine—fresh air, sunlight, and sky—laughter, gossip, and small talk. Sure, we'll talk about Trump, Truth, and Trudeau, but also that outfit Grimes wore last night on Instagram. Sure, we'll talk about Injustice, Impermanence, and Imperialism, but also blue butterflies from Baie-d'Urfé, purple tomatoes from Santropol Roulant, and bison burgers from Else's.

There's nothing we won't throw on the campfire of our conversation, nothing we won't sacrifice on the altar, nothing that won't be offered up as a burnt offering to the God of Talk, a deity who delights in frivolity and fanfare, a deity whose Holy of Holies can be found wherever people gather to tweet like parakeets, and groom each other like chimpanzees, a deity who can see the beauty in the pointless privileged prattle of a Jane Austen novel.

11.

Asshole Magnet

"The problem with Taleb is not that he's an asshole. He is an asshole. The problem with Taleb is that he is right."—Dan from Prague

"Know what you are, John? You're an asshole magnet." She said other mean stuff (as did I), but I've forgotten the rest. We were in the middle of that particularly painful part of the break-up ritual. When the sweet wine of love turns into bitter vinegar in your mouth. When the potion you and Isolde quaffed a lifetime ago turns into a kind of Tourette's-inducing truth serum, and we fall into an epileptic fit of compulsive truth-telling.

It's taken me a couple of decades to realize this, but she was right about me. I do in fact have a lot of highly disagreeable friends. But this isn't by design; it's an unfortunate side-effect, the unavoidable byproduct of a lifelong love affair with courage. No virtue charms me more. But every love comes at a cost, even the love of a virtue; and alas, the courageous are often disagreeable and sometimes reckless. It goes with the territory.

We say "*de gustibus non est disputandum*" (there's no accounting for taste) when we're feeling cornered and embarrassed (e.g., when someone discovers your Céline Dion CDs, your kitten calendars, your extensive collection of vintage garden gnomes). We say it when we're feeling lazy or wish to avoid conflict (e.g., you say "tow-may-tow" and I'll say "tow-mah-tow"). We say it when we do not wish to defend that which we dimly suspect to be indefensible. Why do we frequently find it hard to give a rational account of our aesthetic judgments? I'm not sure. But I know it applies to our taste in people just as much as our taste in music, calendars, and collectibles.

Just as there are hot people who leave us cold, there are good people who we respect immensely but avoid socially. Love and friendship often march to the beat of unseen drummers. When pressed by a modern-day Socrates, I find it very hard, at times, to justify my seemingly eclectic taste in friends. Most of the time, I really couldn't tell you why I gravitate toward the one, avoid the other. All I can say with certainty is that it's got something to do with a highly idiosyncratic estimation of a person's character.

I can tolerate some pretty major flaws in my friends, flaws that others find insufferable, and yet there's one relatively minor vice, stinginess, which I find thoroughly repulsive. My estimation of the virtues is equally uneven. I find, time and again, that I am partial to particular virtues, such as courage. Moral clarity's great but courage is better; because your heart can be in the right place, but if your balls aren't, you probably won't do the right thing when it matters.

12.

In Praise of Bullying

"Trump is the first asshole president—like, openly an asshole. And there's so many guys out there that are assholes—who wanna support another asshole—and they're all, like: 'Finally, one of us!'"—Joe Rogan, *The Joe Rogan Experience* (October 2, 2019)

In *Becoming* (2018), Michelle Obama describes how she dealt with a girl who was bullying her incessantly when she was a kid. Did she expect an adult in her Southside Chicago neighborhood to intervene? Nope. Did she look to an authority figure to solve her problem? Nope. One day, after a particularly nasty remark, she lunged at the bully. They rolled around in the dirt for a minute or two, punching and kicking each other like crazy until someone stepped in and broke up the fight. After that, the bullying stopped. She'd won the bully's respect. What's more, she'd made it clear that she wasn't to be messed with.

I was also bullied as a kid. He was an older kid named Ricky Flood. And he terrorized me. But he also taught me some invaluable lessons, such as: (1) the importance of not walking around with a "KICK ME" sign you put on your own back; (2) the futility and stupidity of trying to go it alone; (3) the futility and stupidity of expecting authority figures to solve all of your problems for you; (4) the importance of building alliances with trustworthy people who will have your back when it matters; (5) the importance of loyalty, promise-keeping, and having your friend's back, especially when it costs you something. On balance, I think I probably learned more from the bullies who kicked the shit out of me when I was a kid than I learned from any of my elementary school teachers.

Look, I know I'm supposed to believe that we've created a far superior world for our children. But sometimes I wonder: Have we? Don't get me wrong, the advantages of our way of doing things are obvious (so there's no reason to recount them here). The drawbacks are less obvious though, and probably more insidious. I sometimes fear that we may be inadvertently raising a generation of young people who don't know how to manage conflict and deal with bullies, a generation of young people who expect authority figures to solve all of their problems for them. What could possibly go wrong?

Well, if Chris Rock is to be believed, a whole lot could go wrong. In his *Netflix* special *Tamborine* (2018), the iconoclastic comedian maintains that: "School is supposed to prepare you for life. Life has assholes. And you should learn how to deal with them as soon as possible. . . . We need bullies. How the fuck you gonna have a school without bullies? Bullies do half the work. Teachers do one half, bullies do the whole other half. And that's the half you're gonna use if you're a fucking grownup. . . . We need fucking bullies. Shit, that's how Trump became president. That's exactly what happened. We got rid of bullies. A real bully showed up, and nobody knew how to handle him."

What's more sustainable: an anti-bullying campaign that teaches kids that they shouldn't stick up for each other and intervene, that they should run and tell an adult whenever something goes wrong? Or an anti-bullying campaign that teaches kids to stand up for the weak and stand up to the strong, an anti-bullying campaign that teaches them to seek out adult help only as a last resort? The gay kids don't need to have the school administration looking out for them 24/7 when they've got loyal friends who love them and are willing to stick up for them. Am I saying we should let kids go all *Lord of the Flies* on each other? Of course not. My ideal schoolyard, much like my ideal economy, is about 90% laissez-faire and 10% regulation. We need to identify and protect those kids who get bullied for days and days until they commit suicide. But we also need to give kids a chance to work things out on their own.

13.

Friend Prostitutes

"NEW RULE: Let's call therapists what they really are: friend prostitutes. Because when a friend tells you to see a therapist, it's just their way of saying 'I don't care about your breakup. Why don't you rent someone who does.'"—Bill Maher, *Real Time with Bill Maher* (February 17, 2018)

There are scenes that stick with you long after you've forgotten the rest of the movie. This scene, from *Crash* (2004), is one of them. Sandra Bullock is crumpled up in pain at the bottom of the stairs. It's not life-threatening but she can't get up. Clearly something's broken. She calls 9-11 but to no avail. They're dealing with a multi-car pile-up and won't be able to get to her for hours.

The operator says she should have a friend drive her to Emergency. So she calls her friends and her husband. But they're all too busy, or can't be bothered. She's finally helped by her Mexican maid. The scene's message is clear: this woman's rich, she lives in a mansion, her husband's the mayor of L.A., and yet she's utterly alone in the world. She has no friends. Not even one.

The basic problem that bedevils us, avers Epicurus, is anxiety about the future. Having friends who we know we can depend upon in times of need, friends who we can lean on if need be, helps to alleviate this anxiety. Friendship bonds are signed in an invisible ink legible only by the light of a really bad day. But if you've got money in our society, you can pay people to do many of the things that are normally done for free by family and friends. For instance, if you're going through a rough patch, you can pay a therapist to help you get through this difficult period. But is this really such a good thing? I don't think so.

Although we spend billions on it, talk therapy seems to help, at best, one in four. Numerous studies have demonstrated this: it simply does not work for most people. What's odd, to my mind, is that nobody who knows what they're talking about seems to dispute this, not even the profession's most vocal apologists. And yet for some strange reason, our collective faith in the promise of therapeutic salvation remains stronger now, perhaps, than ever before.

Despite this abysmal track record, most of us reflexively advise our friends and relatives to "get some help" when they're going through a tough time. Most of us believe, in a lazy, unthinking way, that seeing a therapist whenever life hurts is, well, you know, just what normal people do. The 1950s viewed getting milk from your mother's breast much as we view getting therapy from your friend's kitchen table.

Those who fail to seek professional help when they're "in a bad place" are viewed with suspicion. At best, we think them eccentric, quirky, and odd, like that weird old friend who still doesn't have a driver's license at 43, or that funny middle-aged aunt who lives alone, makes her own hummus, and refuses to use underarm deodorant. At worst, we begin to resent their refusal: "I can't believe she *still* hasn't seen someone! I mean, seriously, at this point, I'm starting to think she wants to be miserable." "Ya, I know what you mean, my brother's the same way. It's like he just doesn't wanna be happy."

Peer pressure to "get help" can be surprisingly strong in the 21st-century West. We've probably all found ourselves in its orbit at some point or another; but none have felt the terrible tug of its gravitational force more than the parents of bratty kids and troubled teens. Most give in to the zeitgeist's demands regardless of whether or not they think it's going to help. And they are richly rewarded for their conformity: they and their wayward children shall be washed in therapeutic grace. Schoolyard sins shall be forgiven. These parents—who get their little monsters "the help they need"—are deemed decent, upstanding, responsible, virtuous, and good. But those who stubbornly refuse to seek professional help for their problematic offspring are subjected to a tsunami wave of righteous indignation.

If Dante was reincarnated today as a mommy-shaming helicopter parent, my guess is that he'd reserve a particularly nasty place in his new and improved *Inferno* for suburban heretics who refuse to find therapists for their difficult kids. These parental outlaws will share a spot on Hell Crescent with crackheads who gave their kids beer for breakfast, working parents who slipped peanut butter sandwiches into school lunches, and that coked-up celebrity who sped down the highway in a red convertible with an unsecured baby on his lap.

Of course all of this social pressure to "get help" is predicated on the assumption that therapy works—that it can fix you, fix your kid, fix your marriage—however, as I mentioned from the outset, numerous studies have demonstrated that therapy simply *does not* work for most people. Some find healing, no doubt about that; but most of those who show up broken, leave broken. That being said, my concern, here, isn't, first and foremost, with whether or not therapy works; it's with therapy's side-effects.

I suspect that many of those who find healing in the therapist's office trade in old problems for new ones. What's worse, I suspect that many who show up broken, leave *more* broken. There are three reasons for this: (1) talk therapy often erodes social skills; (2) most talk therapy is based upon a discredited model of the mind; and (3) talk therapy often undermines friendship.

1. *How Talk Therapy Erodes Social Skills:* Although some learn how to communicate more effectively in therapy, most do not. All to the contrary, talk therapy usually reinforces many of the same inept ways of relating, such as a monological manner, which contributed to the individual's social isolation in the first place. Good conversation is based on give-and-take, dialogue, empathy, reciprocity, and giving a shit about how the other person feels. When you're talking with a friend, even an extremely close friend, you're always trying, to some extent, to engage them, to be funny and entertaining. But when you're talking with your therapist, it's all about you—and that's, well, not that good for you.

2. *Talk Therapy is Based on a Discredited Model of the Mind:* We live in a therapeutic culture that's been extolling the virtues of venting for the better part of a century. As such, we've all heard a great deal about the need to express our anger and talk, at length, about things that have made us angry in the past. All of this is based upon a hydraulic model of the mind that was popularized during the Industrial Revolution, a model that still relies heavily—perhaps unsurprisingly—upon steam-engine metaphors (e.g., pressure build-up, the importance of pressure-release valves, etc.). But since we're dealing here with the received wisdom of our age, this underlying rationale is rarely made manifest, nor is it subjected to serious scrutiny.

Most of us simply assume that venting is good for us. What's more, we assume that its benefits have been proven (somewhere) and backed up by solid research. In fact, the rationale for venting is based upon a hydraulic model of the mind which researchers disproved and discarded decades ago. As Susan Cain puts it in *Quiet* (2012): "The 'catharsis hypothesis' — that aggression builds up inside us until it's healthily released — dates back to the Greeks, was revived by Freud, and gained steam during the 'let it all hang out' 1960s of punching bags and primal screams. But the catharsis hypothesis is a myth — a plausible one, an elegant one, but a myth nonetheless. Scores of studies have shown that venting doesn't soothe anger; it fuels it." Talking about your problems can make them worse.

3. *Talk Therapy Undermines Friendship:* We all like going out for dinner from time to time, and this usually involves paying a stranger to cook for us. Still, most of our meals are home-cooked by family members or friends. But imagine, for a moment, how strange it would be if we all ate out at restaurants so much that we forgot how to cook for each other. What's more, imagine if we came to believe that it was actually dangerous and unhealthy for "non-professionals" to cook for themselves and others. That, to my mind, is where we are right now vis-à-vis therapy in our culture. Many of us seem to have come to the conclusion that the normal thing to do—Plan A, as it were—is to go to a therapist whenever something's wrong. And that's the problem. *That's* what's stunting the growth of our personal relationships and rendering so many of our friendships shallow and superficial.

In *The Commercialization of Intimate Life* (2003), sociologist Arlie Russell Hochschild maintains that an over-reliance upon therapy is one of liberal feminism's greatest weaknesses: "While books like *Women Who Love Too Much* focus on therapy, ironically the actual process of healing is subtracted from the image of normal family or communal bonds. The women in Norwood's tales seem to live in a wider community strikingly barren of emotional support. Actual healing is reserved for a separate zone of paid professionals where people have PhDs, MDs, MAs, accept money, and have special therapeutic identities. While psychotherapy is surely a help to many, it is no substitute for life itself. In the picture Norwood paints, there is little power of healing outside of therapy. In the stories Norwood tells, love doesn't heal. When you give it, it doesn't take. When another offers it, it may feel good but it's not good for you. . . . If the word 'therapy' conveys the desire to help another to get to the root of a problem, this is a very deep subtraction from our idea of love and friendship. It thins and lightens our idea of love. We are invited to confine our trust to the thinner, once-a-week, 'processed' concern of the professional. This may add to our expectations of therapy, but it lightens our expectations of lovers, family, and friends."

Though some of our deepest and most meaningful connections to others grow out of joy, most are forged in adversity: e.g., she was there for me when I was going through that terrible break-up; she was there, as well, when my mother was dying of cancer; he was there for me when I got fired; he was there, as well, when I was recovering from that horrible car accident. Every time you pay someone to hang out with you during a rough patch, you rob yourself of an opportunity to get closer to a friend or relative.

I once took a powerful course of antibiotics that wreaked havoc on my digestive system for months. Do I regret taking the antibiotics? Of course not. But I wish I had been better informed about how much damage "the cure" would do. Likewise, it's time to have an honest conversation about the sociological side-effects of talk therapy. We need to start viewing talk therapy the way we've come to view antibiotics. Only a fool would say that antibiotics are useless. Likewise, only a fool would say that talk therapy is useless. But we now know that antibiotics have been vastly over-prescribed, and that this overuse has done real damage. What's more, we now know that even when the use of antibiotics is warranted, there are harmful side-effects associated with their use which need to be acknowledged and addressed. The same is no doubt true of talk therapy.

14.

Worst Date Ever

"Don't worry about people's profiles. Find somebody who you think is cute enough, and go and interact with them as soon as possible. Because the way that people naturally evaluate physical chemistry is through how an interaction makes them feel. We don't choose partners the way that we choose furniture. Because furniture doesn't have to choose us back. But partners do."—Benjamin Karney, *Ologies Podcast* (February 12, 2019)

I met her at a party in my late teens. Let's call her Sheila. We hit it off spectacularly and talked till dawn. Even scaled Mount Royal to watch the sunrise. Yeah, it was *that* romantic, *that* perfect. But then she had to go. Had to catch her ride back to Sherbrooke. After making out like the end of the world was nigh, we exchanged phone numbers and made future plans. I was gonna take the bus down to Sherbrooke the following weekend. We swore off profane communication methods such as the telephone. Such was the sacredness of our connection, and our ardent desire to preserve its sanctity: "Just call me when you get there, John. Call me from the station."

And that's just what I did a week later. One of her five roommates answered. When she told Sheila who it was I distinctly remember hearing a muffled "Oh, fuck!" But she came to the station regardless. After a decidedly cool reception, she took me back to her apartment. I recall that it resembled a doctor's office: a large living room with six bedrooms, a bathroom, and a kitchen spoking off its perimeter.

Clearly she wasn't psyched to see me but I couldn't figure out why. Whatever. I can take a hint. I called the bus station to see when the next bus back to Montreal was leaving. Fuck! Not till tomorrow morning. I'm stuck here. Fuck! After a moment of self-loathing, I decided to make the best of it. I befriended her roommates and went out for beers and burgers at the local pub. We were eventually joined by Sheila and half the city. It really was a great place: live music, great beer, fantastic food, the works.

At some point, I saw Sheila making out with some Greek god of a man on the dance floor. They were inseparable for the rest of the night. After the bar closed, I returned to the apartment with her roommates, my new best friends, and they set me up on a couch in the living room. I crashed immediately. But I didn't stay asleep long. Because Sheila and the Greek god came home and had loud sex, over and over again, all night long; and, as luck would have it, my couch was right up against her bedroom wall. It was a long night.

15.

Romantic Interlude III: Scrabble, Ecstasy, & Fertility Clinics

David Fiore and I pushed our nocturnal proclivities to the limit that semester. Went weeks and weeks without seeing the sun. We'd sleep all day, read and write all night, and meet for a game of Scrabble at three in the morning. Scrabble, ecstasy, and fertility clinics: so much human, all-too-human striving. And yet I can't help but wonder: Were we pushing the limits of human nature or trying to figure out where they might be?

I was dying for a good game of Scrabble as I sat there in the fertility clinic, waiting for some stranger to stick a giant needle into my nuts. Of course they told me to wait, the doctor told me to take it easy. But I didn't because I was 29, and, like most guys in their twenties, I still secretly suspected that I was a superhero. So I carried that kid, popped the stitches, and that's why the vasectomy can't be reversed.

And that's why I'm sitting here in this stupid waiting room, under these stupid fluorescent lights, reading these stupid magazines filled with stupid questionnaires. The one on Page 18 says it comes down to this: "Are you a dog person or a cat person?"

"Dude," said Jimmy, "could swear I just saw a big lizard walking across your living room floor."

The sun was coming up, we were coming down, and Samantha, the four-and-a-half-foot-long iguana who lived with us, was making her way like a snob to the windowsill to bathe in the morning light.

Jenny giggled to herself: "Bees are so furry and cute up close. They're like little kitty cats, flying brainwashed kitty cats, living in totalitarian societies."

Jimmy nodded in agreement: "And moths are butterflies on crack who flunked flight school."

Scrabble, ecstasy, and fertility clinics: so much human, all-too-human striving. And yet I can't help but wonder: Were we pushing the limits of human nature or trying to figure out where they might be?

The grownup me wants to march right back in time and protest in front of each one of these magical moments with a placard that reads: IT WON'T WORK! HERE'S WHY. But then Joy wells up within me, laughs, and says it already has.

PART IV

SURFACES AND ESSENCES

Last time I saw my brother, he smelled bad. Really bad. Don't think he'd washed in a week. Maybe two. His hair was greasy and matted. Teeth were yellow. Clothes were stained. He wore mismatched socks and his t-shirt was inside-out. It was painful to behold: the depression was killing him.

He died a few days later. Suicide.

I realize now, and only in retrospect, that the signs were all there. When someone loses the will to look good, it's often because they've begun to lose the will to live. Anyone who's worked with the elderly will tell you this (e.g., we knew Mrs. Johnson's days were numbered when she stopped putting on her make-up in the morning, and we knew Mrs. Cooper wasn't long for this world when she stopped curling her hair).

Like most of you, I was vain in my teens and early twenties. But I was vain with a bad conscience. It felt like a character flaw. Something shameful. Something to be hidden from view. It's a kind of hypocrisy that's pretty much the norm in our culture. As Nassim Nicholas

Taleb rightly observes: "Most of what they call humility is successfully disguised arrogance."[1]

I used to despise vanity in myself and others. But at 45, I must confess that I've warmed to it. Indeed, I've come to see the wisdom in something Benjamin Franklin said (something, truth be told, which I once found perverse): "Most people dislike vanity in others, whatever share they have of it themselves; but I give it fair quarter wherever I meet with it, being persuaded that it is often productive of good to the possessor, and to others that are within his sphere of action; and therefore, in many cases, it would not be altogether absurd if a man were to thank God for his vanity among the other comforts of life."[2]

1. Nassim Nicholas Taleb, *The Bed of Procrustes* (2016).
2. Benjamin Franklin, *The Autobiography of Benjamin Franklin* (1791).

16.

In Praise of Golddiggers

He's a self-made millionaire, a grey-haired man in his early fifties. She's twenty-eight and drop-dead gorgeous. We watch them, and judge them, as they get out of the red Ferrari and walk into the trendy restaurant on boulevard Saint-Laurent—you know, the one on the east side of the street, just north of Sherbrooke. Those of us who judge the rich guy do so because we think he's a creepy lecher who should be with someone his own age. For god's sake, look at her! She could be his daughter!

Whatever we make of the rich guy, and his intentions, our judgement of the bombshell on his arm is invariably harsher. It's harsher, in part, because anyone with the emotional maturity of a twelve-year-old knows that using people is wrong. We all know, spontaneously, without analyzing, that Kant was on to something when he said that we should never treat another human being like an instrument, like a means to an end. We look at the rich guy and something within us wants to cry out: "You fool, you stupid fool! Can't you see what's going on here? She's only with you for the money!" But what if we've got it all wrong? What if she loves him, really loves him, and not for his money, but for who he is?

What if he tried dating the blue-blooded daughters of the North American elite? What if these Ivy-League-educated trust-fund gals found all of his talk about business and bling boring? What if they found his intense preoccupation with status graceless, gauche, and gross? What if they found his obsession with money thoroughly unattractive? And what if he found their company and conversation equally nettlesome? What if all they wanted to talk about, over fair-trade coffee at Starbucks, was books, boring books, and documentaries, *tedious* documentaries, about suffering, suffering in faraway places he can't pronounce? What if they went on and on, till he thought he was going to bleed out through the eyes, about that fucking long weekend they spent in the Third World volunteering for an NGO?

What if the golddigger on his arm is the first woman he's met who really appreciates all of the sacrifices he's had to make to get to where he is? What if she's the first woman he's met who loves money and status as much as he does? What if their relationship is actually based on a solid foundation of shared values, profound respect, and mutual understanding (they're both golddiggers, after all)? What if they're in love—*really* in love? My guess is that they almost always are. And that's a beautiful thing, really it is. Because everyone needs to find love in this broken and burning world. And yet so few of us do. So when we see two people who *have* momentarily found love, "what we do," writes Tony Hoagland, "is natural: we take our burned hands out of our pockets, and clap."[1]

Perfect people are rare, perfect pairings are not; you don't have to be perfect to be perfect for each other.

1. Tony Hoagland, "Grammar," *Donkey Gospel* (1998).

17.

Hiding in Plain Sight

If you've seen *Catch Me If You Can* (2003), you know how easy it is to fool people when you look the part. What's less obvious is that the opposite is often equally true. People like me, who've been fooled one too many times by smooth-talking charlatans in suits, are often overly critical of anybody who looks the part, and overly trusting of unkempt vulgarians. But alas, exceptionally good con artists have always known this.

Jean-Jacques Rousseau mastered the art of playing rich people. An impressive feat, when you think about it, because rich people are surrounded at all times by a cloud of people who are trying to play them. How did he do it? By playing the part of the uncouth but thoroughly down-to-earth guy who just doesn't give a fuck. It's a well-worn ploy. At least as old as Romanticism. And we ignore its allure at our peril. Protecting yourself from the Frank Abagnales of this world is important. But it's also good to remember that being rough around the edges can be an integral part of a charlatan's shtick.

We were raised to believe that common sense is the enemy, things are never what they seem, and judging a book by its cover is the worst thing you can do. This obsession with depths has made it possible for some straightforwardly sketchy people to hide in plain sight. Louis

CK is a case in point. We stupidly assumed that a man who talks about what a pervert he is all the time, in public, couldn't possibly be a pervert in real life. I suspect that Trump slipped under the radar for many of the same reasons.

Most people are exactly what they seem to be. That nice guy at work with the perfect teeth: he might be a monster who secretly kills kittens for fun, but he's probably just a nice guy with perfect teeth. That rude asshole you met online: he might be a misunderstood genius with a heart of gold, but he's probably just a rude asshole. More often than not, if it looks like a duck, it's a duck. And if it looks like a schmuck, talks like a schmuck, and walks like a schmuck, it's a schmuck.

*

In nature, bright colors are often a warning: I'm poisonous! Don't eat me! Stay away! Insect-eating birds avoid any butterfly who looks like a monarch, intelligent residents of the Amazon refrain from handling poison dart frogs, and only a fool would eat that bright red mushroom in the meadow. However, in the forest of social life, bright colors are often an invitation: I'm friendly, gregarious, approachable, somewhat outrageous, thoroughly interesting, and definitely not poisonous.

My friend Janice Simpkins taught me a handy heuristic based on this insight, which has served me well on numerous occasions: "If you find yourself stranded in a room full of strangers—at some social function—talk to the person wearing the loudest outfit, because that person is invariably the friendliest person in the room."

But alas, in nature and in social life, we sometimes encounter false advertising. Biologists call it mimicry. For instance, the red milk snake (*Lampropeltis triangulum syspila*) is not poisonous, nor is the equally harmless scarlet kingsnake (*Lampropeltis elapsoides*). Yet predators steer clear of them both because they look like the deadly coral snake (*Micrurus fulvius*).

Likewise, in social life, we sometimes encounter brightly colored bores (e.g., middle-class hipsters who dress like bohemians but talk like accountants). The sense of betrayal that washes over you when you find yourself stuck in a pointless conversation with one of these philistines is surprisingly intense: their mimicry seems to offend our innate sense of social justice. Brightly colored bores should come with a warning. Something like this:

WARNING: OBJECTS BEHIND
THIS INTERESTING PERSONA
ARE DULLER THAN THEY APPEAR

18.

On Being Yourself

"The liberal story cherishes human liberty as its number one value. It argues that all authority ultimately stems from the free will of individual humans, as expressed in their feelings, desires, and choices. In politics, liberalism believes that the voter knows best. It therefore upholds democratic elections. In economics, liberalism maintains that the customer is always right. It therefore hails free-market principles. In personal matters, liberalism encourages people to listen to themselves, be true to themselves, and follow their hearts—as long as they do not infringe on the liberties of others. This personal freedom is enshrined in human rights."—Yuval Noah Harari, *21 Lessons for the 21st Century* (2018)

My first serious girlfriend said that her motto, the creed which she lived by, was "go with the flow" (indeed, it was her high-school yearbook quote). She was (and is) such a sweet person. Such a good person: kind, loving, patient, wise. But, truth be told, I remember being viscerally repulsed by her yearbook quote, and, since I was arrogant and obnoxious at sixteen, I probably told her as much. Probably said something really mean. Something I've conveniently forgotten. Regardless, I remember thinking that even though my life was a complete mess, even though I was flunking out of school, even though I was totally confused, even though I was angry all the time for no good reason, even though I had no idea what I wanted to do with my life, I could, nevertheless, be sure of at least one thing: I did *not* want to go with the flow!

Much of my twenties were consumed by a quixotic (and, in retrospect, rather ridiculous) attempt to live a life less ordinary. But when I look back now, at all that crazy counter-cultural stuff I did, I find that most of it was shockingly ordinary. When I swap war-stories with people my age, after a few beers, we invariably discover that we've got the same twenty stories from our twenties. Buddy of mine calls them twin tales. Because they're so hard to tell apart. Proper nouns being their only distinguishing feature. Coming to terms with your own ordinariness is a bitter pill to swallow when you've been raised to believe that originality is a cardinal virtue. But it's a bitter pill that most of us have swallowed. After all, the commonplace nature of my generation's counter-cultural war-stories is hardly their most unflattering feature. The worst thing you can say about us—the thing that many of my friends still fail to acknowledge—is that the crazy counter-cultural stuff we did wasn't particularly counter-cultural.

Nor was it particularly radical. As Thomas Frank makes clear in *The Conquest of Cool* (1997), much of what passes for counter-cultural behavior since the 1960s is in fact an integral part of the "flow" of consumer culture. So I guess you could say that I've been going with the flow for quite some time now, regardless of my intentions and pretensions. Even at the height of my twenties—when I was an obnoxious, self-righteous, left-wing vegan, with blue hair and tattoos—my individual-centered approach to social change pretty much ensured my complicity. As Tony Hoagland puts it at the end of "Hard Rain":

I used to think I was not part of this,
that I could mind my own business and get along,
but that was just another song

that had been taught to me since birth—
whose words I was humming under my breath,
as I was walking thorough the Springdale Mall.[1]

The personal isn't necessarily political. That said, society does benefit when individuals decide to, say, quit smoking, get in shape, or learn how to control their anger. But the benefits accrue primarily to the individual in question. Those close to the individual—such as partner, children, family members, close friends—also benefit; however, outside of that sacred circle, the benefits are largely negligible. Trying to solve the world's problems with a program of individual-centered perfectionism is like trying to solve the problems of the poor with a program of trickle-down economics.

If the Devil's greatest trick was to convince the world he didn't exist, consumer culture's greatest trick was to convince us that we could be radical without being political. The people running this system aren't threatened by your tribal tattoos, your hard-core haircut, your skateboarding, your edgy music, your veganism, your yoga, your recreational drug use, your bisexuality, your dreads, your piercings, your kinky taste in porn—or anything else you do by yourself, or with other consenting adults, in the privacy of your own home. You may see a radical subculture, but they just see another niche market.

*

If a time machine like the one described in David Fiore's *Hypocritic Days* (2014) was discovered tomorrow, and I was asked to write a travel brochure for the 21st-century West next week, I'd be sure to mention individualism as one of our era's big attractions. The freedom to *be yourself*, do your own thing, choose your own profession, move to a new place, break with tradition, make a new family, be a little weird, have a little privacy: we take these things for

1. Tony Hoagland, "Hard Rain," *Hard Rain* (2005).

73

granted far too often. Many of our ancestors would kill for what we have. Many of mine died for it. Many of yours did too.

Still, individualism is a human thing, and, like all human things, it's flawed. The emancipation of the individual has come at a cost, sometimes a hefty cost. But I would nevertheless argue that the freedom to be yourself is one of our culture's greatest accomplishments. It's well worth fighting for, despite its drawbacks. At some point, however, in the not-so-distant past, we seem to have collectively forgotten what it is that we were fighting for all along, what it really means to be authentic, what it really means to be yourself. And I think I know why. We've confused *being yourself* with *being original*.

If, like Natalie Portman's character in *Garden State* (2004), you think that to be an individual, to be yourself, you've got to "do something that has never, ever been done before . . . throughout human existence," you're bound to go through life profoundly disappointed with yourself. Because this is an unrealistic goal, a silly ideal. You're setting yourself up for failure. We can't *all* be original. Just as there's a limited amount of beachfront property in the world, there's a limited number of people who can be first, unique, singular, and truly original (*sui generis*). To some extent this is a function of the limited number of geniuses in the world. But it's mostly a function of dumb luck: some people just happen to be the first one to think or do something new. After all, *someone* has to be first.

In his classic essay on the subject—"On Thinking for Yourself" (1851)—Schopenhauer stresses that being the first one to think a particular thought isn't what's important. What's important is that you make a thought your own. What's important is that this newly discovered idea enter "into the whole system of your thought" as "an integral part, a living member"; "that it stand in complete and firm relation with what you already know; that it is understood with all that underlies it and follows from it; that it wears the color, the precise shade, the distinguishing mark, of your own way of thinking."[2]

*

In *The Prince* (1532), Machiavelli famously maintains that it's better to be feared than loved. I'm pretty sure my wise old mentor, Ron Walters, had this in mind when he told me, the night before my first job talk: "Remember, John, don't make waves. When it comes to hiring committees, it's better to be liked than loved." In other words, don't be yourself. I've since sat on numerous hiring committees and seen the truth of my mentor's words on countless occasions. Rarely (if ever) do you get your first choice, or even your second choice, when you're sitting on a hiring committee. The candidate who gets the job is usually somebody who everybody liked but nobody loved, somebody who was everybody's third, forth, or fifth choice.

The same is not true in other domains (e.g., politics, religion, literature, activism, moral reform, etc.) wherein zealous minorities have proven far more effective than tepid majorities. In these domains, it's better to be loved than liked. The political impotence of the environmental movement in the second half of the twentieth century is a case in point. Despite widespread support, it was remarkably ineffective because those who cared about the environment invariably cared about something else more (e.g., racism, feminism, abortion, free speech, pornography, terrorism, religion, Wall Street, etc.). Environmentalism was everyone's third, forth, or fifth choice. It was the cause everybody liked but nobody loved.

If you strive to be liked by all, as people-pleasers habitually do, you're probably misrepresenting yourself in big and small ways all the time. You're probably sending out a lot of mixed and confusing signals. And you're probably attracting all sorts of people who aren't

2. Arthur Schopenhauer, *Essays and Aphorisms* (1970). Translated by R. J. Hollingdale.

particularly well-suited to you. This is precisely why people-pleasers so often find themselves surrounded by people they can't stand, people who wouldn't like them much either if they knew them better. If you're looking for love, you can't be someone you're not. If you strive to be liked by all you're sure to be loved by none.

*

"So, if I'm looking for love, I should just be myself, right?" Not necessarily. If you happen to be a thoroughly awesome person, then, by all means, be yourself. But few of us are. Like fixer-uppers on a renovation show, most of us need work. "Being yourself" is rarely the solution and often the problem, especially if you suck. "The future," Haspel wagers, "will marvel that we regarded 'be yourself' as sound moral advice."[3] "Stop being yourself" is sounder advice. "Start being someone else" is even better, though it's often hard for those of us who were raised in the modern West to see why this is the case. If you're reading this book, you probably subscribe to most of what Yuval Noah Harari refers to as "the liberal story". Phrases such as these ring true to you: the voter knows best, the customer is always right, follow your heart, be yourself. The liberal story has taught us to revere the self-sufficiency of heroic individuals who figure things out on their own, and this has made it exceptionally hard for us to see the wisdom of copying, mimicry, and imitation.

If everybody had to brave the dark forest of change alone, and blaze a fresh trail to the other side, few of us would be equal to the task. Thankfully, however, this simply isn't the case. You don't have to go it alone, nor do you have to blaze your own trail. There's a simple shortcut, a time-honored technique, well-known to ancient philosophers like Epictetus: "one of the best ways to elevate your character immediately is to find worthy role models to emulate." Since you have in all likelihood internalized much of the liberal story, aping others in such a deliberate fashion might feel forced,

3. Aaron Haspel, *Everything: A Book of Aphorisms* (2015).

strange, and inauthentic at first. But I encourage you to push through your initial discomfort: "Invoke the characteristics of the people you admire most and adopt their manners, speech, and behavior as your own. There is nothing false in this. We all carry the seeds of greatness within us, but we need an image as a point of focus in order that they may sprout."[4]

4. Epictetus, *The Art of Living* (2013).

19.

The Right to be Stupid

"Everybody gets mad because I say these jokes, but you gotta understand that this is the best time to say them. More now than ever, and I know there's some comedians in the back. Motherfucker, you have a responsibility to speak recklessly. Otherwise my kids may never know what reckless talk sounds like. The joys of being wrong. I didn't come here to be right, I just came here to fuck around."—Dave Chappelle, *The Bird Revelation* (2017)

Male rapacity and female vulnerability are taken for granted in the neo-Victorian society depicted in Neal Stephenson's sci-fi classic *The Diamond Age* (1995). Surveillance drones ensure that women like Nell, the novel's protagonist, are never alone with men. Wherever they go, the hovering chaperone pods are there: searching for possible signs of male misbehavior, safeguarding feminine virtue, and documenting everything. "By the time she had reached the gates of the Academy, the chaperone pod had gathered enough evidence to support a formal sexual harassment accusation, should Nell have wished to bring one."[1] Is this our future? I certainly hope not.

Although I refuse to take male rapacity and female vulnerability for granted, I must confess that, alas, at times, it's a theory that seems

1. Neal Stephenson, *The Diamond Age: Or, a Young Lady's Illustrated Primer* (1995).

to fit the facts. Early in my teaching career, profs told me, with some regularity, that they found it hard to resist the urge to ogle their students. I was always mystified by this—because I find it very easy to refrain from checking out teenage girls, just as I found it very easy to refrain from checking out my little sisters when we were growing up, just as I find it very easy to "hold it" and not piss myself when I've gotta go but have yet to find a bathroom.

The ability to effortlessly repress drives and focus our sexuality and aggression on appropriate people is central to what it means to be a civilized grownup. When we see an older kid who's still in diapers, we don't say "well, you know, it's natural to piss yourself whenever you feel the need to pee", we say: "Why isn't that kid potty-trained yet?" Likewise, when I meet a middle-aged lecher who can't stop eye-fucking every teenage girl he sees, I don't say, "well, you know, it's natural", I say: "Shouldn't your face be potty-trained by now?"

I'm well aware of the problem of sexual misconduct on campus. I got my job at John Abbott College because a pervy prof was ousted mid-semester and they were desperately in need of an immediate replacement. I'll spare you the gory details about the pervy prof's misdeeds. Suffice it to say that what he was doing, he was doing to, and in some cases with, minors. This kind of thing is seriously gross and obviously wrong. It's also against the law. Faculty who mess around with minors deserve what's coming to them. But if the student in question is over 18, and we're talking about a consensual relationship between two voting adults, things aren't nearly so clear.

Therapists are taught to beware of "erotic transference"—that is, the process whereby a client develops romantic feelings for his or her therapist. Teachers should be taught to beware of a similar phenomenon (but, in my experience, they rarely are). Pedagogy is often suffused with a kind of erotic energy. When you're falling in love with a subject, or an idea, it's fairly easy to fall in love with the person who's teaching it to you. Wise teachers have always known this.

Near the end of Plato's *Symposium*, Alcibiades shows up to the party wasted and regales Agathon's guests with a story. When he was a teenager, he became obsessed with one of his teachers—a guy named Socrates—who introduced him to "the madness and Bacchic frenzy of philosophy". There was something bewitchingly beautiful about his speech: "I was struck and bitten by the words of philosophy, which cling on more fiercely than a snake." Before long, Alcibiades is in love with Socrates.

Alcibiades tries to seduce Socrates on a few occasions. His shamelessness is astounding, as is his nerve. But he fails each and every time because Socrates knows himself and the pedagogical process far too well. He knows that hooking up with a teenage student is a really bad idea. Just as he knows that Alcibiades has in fact fallen in love, not with him, but with philosophy. Whereas immature teachers are happy to let you mistake the message for the man, wise teachers like Socrates cultivate a healthy distance. But what if teachers fail to cultivate a healthy distance? Should they be fired? Thrown in jail? Or merely frowned upon?

Many companies forbid their employees from being romantically involved with their direct supervisor. Because the conflicts of interest are virtually inescapable. Thinking along similar lines, it seems reasonable for universities to insist that faculty refrain from dating students presently enrolled in their classes. But aside from that specific situation, is it right to legislate what adults can and cannot do on their own time? I think not. Well-intentioned legislation of this kind infantilizes the very women (and, at times, men) it seeks to save. It treats individuals who are old enough to drink, vote, and marry like helpless little children—devoid of agency and desperately in need of institutional protection. How is this empowering? How is it emancipatory? And in what universe is it feminist?

In "Professors, Power and Predators: Why Student-Teacher Relationships Should Be Banned," Toula Drimonis maintains that student-teacher relationships should be banned outright because they're fraught with power imbalances.[2] I must confess that I initially thought this was a good idea. But I've had a change of heart. To some extent, this is because I know so many happily married couples that started out as student-teacher relationships.

Fred Bode and Janice Simpkins, two of my closest friends in the world, met and fell in love when she was an undergraduate and he was a professor at Concordia University. They've been happily married for well over 40 years. As Laura Kipnis rightly observes in *Unwanted Advances: Sexual Paranoia Comes to Campus* (2017), you can't throw a stone on a North American campus without hitting a couple of this kind. They are very common. Outlawing a practice that seems to work out well with some regularity seems at best bizarre. Yet this is exactly what Emma Healey would have us do.

In "Stories Like Passwords," Emma Healey describes a relationship she had with a guy she was dating on and off for two years when she was an undergraduate and he was a professor at Concordia University. The age difference between her and her boyfriend was approximately the same as the age difference between my friends Fred and Janice: she was 19 and he was 34. Just as my friend Janice was never actually registered in any of Fred's classes, Healey was never actually registered in any of her boyfriend's classes. Yet she now maintains that their entire relationship was "literally criminal" because of the power imbalance.[3]

Are student-teacher relationships fraught with power imbalances?

2. Toula Drimonis, "Professors, Power and Predators: Why Student-Teacher Relationships Should Be Banned," *Canada's National Observer* (January 17, 2018).
3. Emma Healey, "Stories Like Passwords," *The Hairpin* (October 6, 2014).

My guess is that most of the time they are. Are these power imbalances potentially problematic? Of course. But isn't this a regular feature of the dating landscape? People with lots of power date the less powerful all the time. A high-powered lawyer friend of mine is a case in point. She makes about $500,000 a year. Her boyfriend, a personal trainer who lives in a little studio apartment, makes a fraction of what she does. Should she dump him because of the power imbalance? Of course not! They're very much in love. Could that power imbalance complicate their relationship at some point? Sure. But that's for them to work out. It's none of our business. The same is true of consensual relationships between students and faculty. If there are power imbalances to contend with, that's for them to work out. It's none of our business. Just as the state has no place in the bedrooms of its citizens, the university has no place in the bedrooms of its employees.

In the wake of #MeToo, we seem to have momentarily forgotten that there's a world of difference between reckless behavior that poses a serious threat to society, such as drunk driving, and idiotic behavior that merely reflects poor judgment, such as eating at McDonald's, dating your ex's sibling, sleeping with your pet tarantula, getting high at work, swimming in Cape Cod's shark-infested waters, buying lottery tickets, licking a metal fence in the middle of the winter, becoming a Scientologist, having unprotected sex with strangers, responding to emails from Nigerian princes, wearing lululemons without underwear, or hooking up with your prof. Just because something's a *really* bad idea, doesn't mean there should be a law forbidding it. The rights and freedoms afforded an adult in a liberal democracy such as ours include the freedom to make bad decisions and the right to be stupid.

20.

Romantic Interlude IV: Summer's Days are Numbered

Then the LORD of Hosts told His Chosen People to get over it already. And my friend's mom did just that. Her face lit up with joy, for the first time in decades, because the undetected early onset Alzheimer's had erased half the entries in that hateful little Naughty List she'd been prayerfully paging through, daily, for longer than she could remember.

Same thing happened to Señor Smartypants, earlier on today, at Abbott, whilst he was waiting in line for the 405 bus. His face lit up with joy, for the first time in weeks, because it was a warm day in April, and he'd forgotten how good sunlight can feel on your face. He closed his eyes and stared at the sun, wondering at the apocalyptic, blood-orange color of eyes wide shut.

Is this what Lot's wife saw, before a jealous God, with a mean streak as long as the Jordan, turned her into a pillar of salt? Did He see red when she saw blood-orange memories of a sinful Sodom she'd grown to love? WE WILL NEVER FORGET and GET OVER IT are easier said than done, LORD. And the life of a wandering Jew isn't for everyone.

Can you really fault her for wanting to put down some roots? Can you really fault her for falling for Sin City? Maybe, like 70-year-old Socrates, she just couldn't bear the thought of leaving. Maybe she was willing to drink her hemlock to make a statement: about disobedient wives, the importance of place, and loyalty to lost causes. Maybe, like Machiavelli, she loved her native city more than her own salty soul. Maybe we have to forget it all, the pleasures and pains of the past, if we wish to really enjoy our brief moment in the sun.

Oh Joseph, Joseph, favored son of Israel, there are times when I see why he loved you best, why he spoiled you rotten, why he indulged your every whim, threw caution to the wind, and dropped a deuceload of denaros on that overpriced coat: you know, the colorful one, that got you into all that trouble: the one you found on eBay and simply *had to have*.

Oh Joseph, Joseph, favored son of Israel: there are times when I find myself reading you as you really ought to be read at all times: slowly and carefully, with the sympathetic ears Jesus had in mind when he cryptically declared: "He that hath ears to hear, let him hear." It's then, and only then, that I get a glimpse, a glorious glimpse, of who you really are. I treasure these moments, these moments when you tip your hand, because they remind me of how much I *get you*, Joseph. And, as you well know, getting someone is almost as great as getting got.

Behind that adorable boyish façade of innocence, behind your effortless small-town decency, and your refusal to succumb to cheap cynicism (which the dimwitted invariably mistake for naïveté), lurks an Old World darkness, a decidedly unAmerican fatalism, and a sadness: the sadness of a broken man, a man who caught a glimpse of something he wasn't supposed to see, something terrible and tragic, intractable and inevitable, at the very heart of human existence. Yours is the inconsolable sadness of a melancholy man who stubbornly refuses to forget how sweet it was to believe in Santa Claus: a man who nevertheless refuses, at one and the same time, to succumb to the siren song of ideology, or the comforting myths of modernity: a man who refuses to fill that Santa-shaped hole with any of its grownup analogs.

And yet, despite all of this, you get up everyday and devote yourself to your wife, your children, and your work, in the full knowledge that it probably won't amount to anything but dust and ashes in the end. Shall I play Adam in the Garden, friend, and call this virtuous beast by its rightful name? Very well then: Her name is Heroism. A shy, understated version of the virtue, to be sure, that feels no burning need to "let it shine" or advertise on LinkedIn.

Even so, I know what's under that bushel of yours, friend. I've seen its warm glow, and recognized its honey light: it's the light of a golden afternoon in late August, an afternoon abuzz with the sweet skyward songs of an angelic army, a heavenly host of winged insects, sent from on high to belt out summer's sumptuous symphony, its soulful swansong, which tells the truth about the Janus-faced nature of these late summer days.

In this garden of earthly delights, this golden green afternoon, an afternoon whose cup runneth over, an afternoon spilling over with life, an afternoon that feels like it could go on forever one moment; and yet, a mere moment later, the very air seems pregnant with the poison-apple knowledge of a forbidden tree. It's not *The* Tree of Knowledge, mind you, the one that gets all the press, the one made famous by the authors of Genesis. It's a lesser-known tree of knowledge: born and raised, this side of Paradise, on the wrong side of the tracks, far from the shadow of grace: a world-weary version of his famous cousin who grew up on the mean streets and favelas that ring The Garden of Eden, God's very first gated community.

He can't tell you much about platonic abstractions like Good and Evil. But he knows a great deal about this fallen world we call home. Today, however, he's got but one sad secret to share: "Summer's days are numbered, friend; Summer's days are numbered." To feel the full weight of your own rapidly approaching death in the midst of this throbbing festival of life is always, it seems, just a little bit more than he can handle. The morbid knowledge weighs on him, as it weighs on you at times.

Perhaps *this* is why his tastiest fruits are always hanging so low to the ground. Perhaps *this* is why he never plays hard to get. And perhaps *this* is why, despite your shyness and your dignity and your reticence, you strive for clarity, shun obscurity, and do not seek to conceal yourself. Alas, I see it clearly now, perhaps for the first time, that you wish to be understood, truly understood. And known. Very well then, friend. Tell me everything. I'd like the long version. "Go back to the beginning. Think about it. Take, if you like, all day."[1]

1. Tony Hoagland, "Poem for Men Only," *Sweet Ruin* (1992).

PART V

LIVING HAPPILY EVERAFTER

Bluebirds have been struck down by her Lutheran singing voice. But when she speaks, ah, when Anna-Liisa speaks, it's music. The words, the sounds, and the silences flow seamlessly, gracefully, hypnotically. What I'm hearing, she tells me, is the embarrassing remnant of an old speech impediment, a source of childhood shame—which a speech therapist, who came highly recommended, failed fully to fix. But I beg to differ, because I hear poetry in her singsong speech. She speaks in cursive writing.

21.

Me Hate You Long Time

"We judge others by their behavior, but we think we have special information about ourselves—we know what we are 'really like' inside, so we can easily find ways to explain away our selfish acts and cling to the illusion that we are better than others."—Jonathan Haidt, *The Happiness Hypothesis* (2006)

Anger often seems to wash over us. We don't choose to get enraged when someone cuts us off in traffic, it just happens. Likewise, we don't choose to flush when someone insults us, nor do we choose to see red when someone screws us over. But these feelings fade with time. They have a half-life. All fires cool and eventually die when they're deprived of fuel. One day you wake up and you're just not that pissed off anymore. You haven't forgotten what happened. And maybe you're not quite ready to forgive. But the memory has lost its sting. If you want to get over it, if you want to be free of your rage, continue along this peaceful path. Let nature take its course. You're on the Road to Recovery. But if the very idea of forgiving them makes you sick, if you're quite sure that you do not want to get over it, come with me. If you want to learn how to be a really good hater, let me show you the way:

Step One: *Fantasize About the Past:* Close your eyes and think about what he or she did to you. And be as specific as possible. What did the sky look like that day? What was on the radio? What were you wearing? Fill the memory up with every last detail. Then replay it in your mind again and again and again, like that song you just can't get enough of. If you do this for a little while, the righteous indignation will well up in you. And you'll feel the change: it's profoundly physiological. Your breathing gets shallow. Your heartbeat quickens. Your palms get sweaty. And your face contorts. As soon as you've whipped yourself up into a white hot rage, move on to Step Two.

Step Two: *Fantasize About the Future:* Okay, now I want you to close your eyes and imagine how you're going to get back at this person, how you're going to get revenge. If you're going to tell them off in front of a room full of people, prepare the speech in your mind. What words are you going to use? Think about how good it's going to feel to humiliate that person, to watch them suffer. It's your revenge fantasy: fill it up with juicy details. And be as specific as possible. Then replay it in your mind again and again and again. Once again, the effects of this perverse form of cognitive behavioral therapy are profoundly physiological: your pupils dilate, a demonic grin spreads across your face, and pleasure centers in your brain are activated. You feel energized, alive, and possessed by a passion that's undeniably pleasant. Presto! As if by magic, you're in hate!

Strange as it may sound, long-term romantic love seems to be sustained by the same willful cognitive processes. We don't choose who we fall in love with. It just happens. That's why the image of Cupid slinging his arrows into the backsides of hapless innocents makes so much intuitive sense to us. You meet someone, lock eyes with them, and—BANG! BOOM! CRASH!—you're powerfully drawn to them. But alas, this kind of intoxicating love fades, like rage, with time. One day you wake up and you're just not "in love" with your partner in that crazy way you were in the beginning. Don't get me wrong, you still love them, you're still attracted to them, and you still want to be with them. It's just that you find it easier and easier to focus on other things (e.g., work, school, friends, family, yourself, etc.).

To some extent this is healthy. But if you're committed to the relationship, if you want to stay with this person, being passive about your love isn't wise. Love can slip through your fingers if you're careless of heart. If you want to be a serial monogamist, go with the flow, let your love fade, and move on to the next flower. But if the very idea of breaking up with Mr. or Mrs. Right makes you sick, if you're quite sure that you do not want to get over this person, come with me. If you want to know how to love somebody long time, let me show you the way:

Step One: *Fantasize About the Past:* Close your eyes and think about all of the good times you've had with this person. And be as specific as possible. What did the sky look like that day? What was on the radio? What were you wearing? Fill up each one of these memories with delicious details. The more the merrier! Then replay these beautiful memories in your mind again and again and again, like that song you just can't get enough of. If you do this for a little while, the magic of love will well up in you. And you'll feel the change: it's profoundly physiological. Your breathing gets deeper. Your heartbeat quickens. And a sweet smile spreads across your face. Now it's time to move on to Step Two.

Step Two: *Fantasize About the Future:* Okay, now I want you to close your eyes and imagine all of the good times you're going to have with this person in the future: vacations, kids, grandchildren, growing old together, and all the rest. Think about how good it's going to feel to be with this particular person for the rest of your life. It's your future, your fantasy: so fill it up with tons of juicy details. And be as specific as possible. Then replay it in your mind again and again and again. Once again, the effects of this cognitive behavioral therapy are profoundly physiological: your pupils dilate, your skin tingles, and your body feels enveloped by a warm glow. You feel energized, alive, and possessed by a passion that's undeniably pleasant. Presto! As if by magic, you're in love!

Eternity isn't about the future, it's about the past. If Heaven is living with the sweet memory of a life well lived, Hell is being trapped in a dank basement room, where you're forced to listen to a record of regrets, on repeat, forever.

22.

Keeping Score

"At a conference on reciprocity, a senior scientist revealed that he kept track on a computer spreadsheet of what he had done for his wife and what she had done for him . . . . The fact that this was his third wife, and that he's now married to his fifth, suggests that keeping score is perhaps not for close relationships."—Frans de Waal, *The Age of Empathy: Nature's Lessons for a Kinder Society* (2010)

Your boss has made it very clear: if you're late for work one more time, you're getting fired. So when you wake up late because of last night's power outage, you're freaking out. Because you need this job. Really need this job. In less than ten minutes, you're out the door and speeding like a demon on the highway. To make your exit, you're forced to cut some guy off. He lays on his horn and yells out horrible obscenities at you. You feel bad about cutting him off, really you do, but you forgive yourself soon after you get to work on time. Because you had a really good reason. Because you need this job. Really need this job. Of course, the guy you cut off doesn't know any of this. And he's red-in-the-face furious, overflowing with righteous indignation. When he gets to work, he tells everyone he knows about the asshole who nearly killed him on the way to work.

Next week, you're driving to work on the same highway—on time, this time—when some asshole rockets past you at an ungodly speed. Wow, you think to yourself, what an inconsiderate, selfish jerk! Doesn't he realize how reckless he's being? A moment later, another asshole cuts you off to make his exit. This time you're furious. You lay on your horn and yell out horrible obscenities at him. You're red-in-the-face furious, overflowing with righteous indignation. When you get to work, you tell everyone you know about the asshole who nearly killed you on the way to work. Of course, the guy who rocketed past you at an ungodly speed doesn't know any of this. He was in a hurry to get to his daughter's school. The principal called him at work to tell him that a freak accident had left his daughter bleeding and unconscious on the gymnasium floor. The other guy—who cut you off to make his exit—was trying to get his pregnant wife to the hospital in time. He felt bad about cutting you off, really he did, but he forgave himself a moment or two after his son was born. Because he had a really good reason: his wife was hemorrhaging severely, and without medical assistance, she and his newborn son might have died.

Like you, I have a self-righteous inner accountant in my head who loves to keep score; loves to keep track of how much I've done for you, how much you've done for me; how much I owe you, how much you owe me. If he graded us solely on what we did and didn't do, you'd at least have a chance (albeit a slim chance) at a fair trial. We'd have to correct for the natural human tendency to see (and remember) *all* the good stuff we do and only *some* of the good stuff others do. Still, if we stuck to the facts, the process might, on occasion, produce a just result. But my self-righteous inner accountant isn't nearly this fair, and yours is probably no better than mine. The lawyer in my head will say anything to win, anything to get me off, anything to make me look good.

What's more, he's been known to cook the books. How? Well, the self-righteous inner accountant in my head grades you only on what you do or don't do. Alas, not so for me: I, like you, get points for what

I do and don't do. But I also get points for good intentions, for being considerate, for good stuff I think about doing. For instance, let's say we're married, and I want you to stop leaving your dirty clothes on the bathroom floor, whilst you want me to stop leaving the toilet seat up. Every time I see myself putting the toilet seat down, I'll smile a self-satisfied smile, pat myself on the back, and give myself some points for being a considerate spouse. But since I'm not you, I won't be there to see you picking up your dirty clothes and putting them in the hamper six days in a row. I will, however, notice the one time you forget to do it. I'll notice that one time, on the seventh day, that you left your dirty clothes in a nasty little pile on the bathroom floor. And when I'm telling you off later on, I'll say that the fact that you failed to pick up after yourself just proves what I've long suspected: namely, that you're a selfish, inconsiderate jerk. Of course you'll indignantly protest: "But I remembered to do it six days in a row, and besides, you left the toilet seat up last night, and I told you how important that was to me!" To which I'll indignantly reply: "But I remembered to put the toilet seat down six days in a row!" Things will, at this point, escalate to screaming and shouting and nowhere nice.

Is there a way out of this familiar story of domestic warfare? I believe there is. All of the truly great wisdom traditions of the world provide us with ways to emancipate ourselves from pointless cycles of resentment and bitterness. From the Roman Stoics, especially Epictetus, we can learn the fine art of forbearance: how to assume the best in those who piss us off, how to be as kind (and forgiving and compassionate) to others as we so often are to ourselves. For instance, if you were driving to work with Epictetus, and some guy cut you off to make his exit, the philosopher would tell you to assume that the guy had a good reason for doing what he did. Maybe his wife's in labor in the backseat. Maybe he just got a horrible call from his daughter's school. Maybe he's gonna get fired if he's late for work. Does this make cutting someone off in traffic okay? Of course not! But assuming the guy had a good reason takes the sting out of it by shutting up your self-righteous inner accountant.

The religious traditions of the world are, at their best, equally good at freeing you from the prison of your own resentment and bitterness. For instance, The Lord's Prayer (Matthew 6:9-13) has Christians the world over reciting these salubrious words on a daily basis: "And forgive us our trespasses, as we forgive them that trespass against us." What's more, the passage is followed up with an explicit warning: "if you do not forgive others their sins, your Father will not forgive your sins" (Matthew 6:15). The strategies to be found are diverse, but they all come down to the same thing: you have to find a way to keep your self-righteous inner accountant in check.

23.

Love Isn't a Liquid Asset

"Don't take it personal, they said; but I did, I took it all quite personal."—Tony Hoagland, "Personal," *Unincorporated Persons in the Late Honda Dynasty* (2010)

David Fennario, a communist playwright I respected immensely when I was a kid, once defined a wealthy WASP as "a guy who loves his dog more than he loves the working class." I remember thinking he was so smart, so brave. In 2001, Ward Churchill, a radical professor many of my graduate school friends respected immensely, sneeringly decried the outpouring of sympathy for the victims of September 11th. They thought he was so smart, so brave. A few years ago, Aadita Chaudhury, an activist many of my colleagues respect immensely, sneeringly decried the outpouring of sympathy for Lindsay Shepherd. They thought she was so smart, so brave. And just last year, Nora Loreto, a journalist I respect immensely, responded similarly to the outpouring of sympathy for the victims of the Humboldt Broncos tragedy. Many of you thought she was so smart, so brave.

Why don't you love the working class as much as you love your dog? Why don't you care about the helpless victims of American foreign policy as much as you care about the helpless victims of the September 11th terrorist attacks? Why are you uninterested in the silencing of students of color but outraged by "white girl tears"? Why are you unmoved by the plight of the victims of the Mosque Massacre, but devastated by the death of a bunch of "white, straight, cisgender male" hockey players? Two faulty assumptions underlie all objections of this kind: (1) love is a scarce resource, and (2) loving is a zero-sum game.

Love is not a scarce resource and loving is not a zero-sum game. Like the Grinch in *How the Grinch Stole Christmas!* (1957), whose "small heart grew three sizes" on Christmas Day, most of us discover that we have much more love to give when we become parents or fall in love. This newfound love isn't a liquid asset that can be readily spent on anyone or anything; it's inextricably tied up in a relationship with a specific person. Likewise, the love we feel for our friends and neighbors isn't a liquid asset that can be readily spent on strangers; it's inextricably tied up in relationships with specific people.

The same is true, alas, of the love we feel for members of our tribe or group. As such, loving is rarely if ever a zero-sum game. As Rousseau rightly observes in *Émile* (1762), the choice, more often than not, isn't between loving *x* and loving *y*; it's between loving *x* and loving nothing: "Every particular society, when it is narrow and unified, is estranged from the all-encompassing society. Every patriot is harsh to foreigners. They are only men. They are nothing in his eyes. This is a drawback, inevitable but not compelling. The essential thing is to be good to the people with whom one lives. . . . Distrust those cosmopolitans who go to great length in their books to discover duties they do not deign to fulfill around them. A philosopher loves the Tartars so as to be spared having to love his neighbors."[1] Should we strive to extend the boundaries of our circle of concern? Absolutely. But is it really all that smart to point out the obvious:

1. Jean-Jacques Rousseau, *Émile: or, On Education* (1762).

namely, that people tend to love what's near more than what's far, and that people tend to love what's familiar more than what's foreign. And is it all that brave to mock people for caring?

24.

The Technology of Trust

"You better watch out / You better not cry / You better not pout / I'm telling you why / Santa Claus is coming to town . . . . He's making a list, / Checking it twice; / Gonna find out who's naughty or nice. . . . He sees you when you're sleeping / He knows when you're awake / He knows if you've been bad or good / So be good for goodness sake."—John Frederick Coots and Haven Gillespie, "Santa Claus is Comin' to Town" (1934)

"Santa Claus is Comin' to Town" has got to be *the* creepiest, as well as the most morally confusing, Christmas carol. In one verse, kids are told that they're supposed to be good because this dirty old man is watching them, NSA-style, 24/7; in the next, they're told they're supposed to be "good for goodness sake." And we wonder why they're so confused. Am I supposed to be good for the reward (that is, the presents)? Am I supposed to be good to avoid punishment? Or am I supposed to do good stuff simply because it's the right thing to do? I was horrified by the idea of an omniscient Big Brother Santa when I was a kid. I remember asking my mom: "Can he see me when I go pee-pee?" As you may or may not already know, Santa's not real; but it looks like his powers may soon be real.

One of the most fascinating episodes of *House*—"The Social

Contract" (S05E17)—tells the story of Nick Greenwald, a well-respected editor at a prestigious press who suddenly loses the ability to tell lies. He simply cannot help but tell people precisely what's on his mind. And the results are disastrous: he insults his boss and tells a bestselling author that his new book sucks, seriously endangering his career; he tells his wife that her interests are silly and she's not that smart, seriously endangering his marriage; and he tells his little girl that she doesn't have an auditory-processing disorder, she's just below average (like her mother), seriously endangering his relationship with his daughter.[1]

If Nick hated his life, all of this truthtelling might be for the best. But he doesn't. All to the contrary, he loves his job, he loves his wife, and he loves his daughter. It's clear that he's horrified, genuinely horrified, by the stupid shit coming out of his mouth, and he's deeply saddened by how much his words are hurting his loved ones. But he just can't stop.

Dr. Gregory House wryly promises to fix Nick Greenwald and return him to his "happy hypocrite" existence in no time. And House delivers. But we can see, from the awkward manner in which Nick and his wife make up after the surgery, that things are never going to be the same between them.

I couldn't help but think of this *House* episode as my friends and I discussed whether or not couples should have each other's passwords. Some say, like the NSA, that if you've got nothing to hide, you've got nothing to fear, whilst others say that people, even married people, have a right to privacy. As for me, well, I couldn't help but remember something Nassim Nicholas Taleb said in *The Bed of Procrustes* (2016): "One of the problems with social networks is that it is getting harder and harder for others to complain about you behind your back."

1. Parts of this chapter appeared first in *Areo*: "The Algorithm Who Loved Me," *Areo* (March 31, 2018).

We need to be able to complain about the people we love in peace. This is probably a human right and definitely a human necessity. Back in the day, of course, all of this bitching and complaining would have taken place in person. It could be overheard only by someone within earshot (hence the term "eavesdropping"). When things went to the telephone things got a little trickier. I'm sure I'm not the only one who's overheard a telephone conversation you wish you hadn't overheard. Even so, if you could find a safe place to chat (and your phones weren't being tapped), a telephone bitch-fest was usually every bit as safe as the old-fashioned face-to-face variety.

But alas, all of this has changed with the advent of texting and email. Ava Gardner was horrified to discover that her billionaire boyfriend Howard Hughes was reading transcripts of all of her conversations. The scene is dramatized in *The Aviator* (2004): Ava Gardner: "You listened to my phone calls?" Howard Hughes: "No! No! No! Honey I would never do that! I'd never do that! I . . . I just read the transcripts, that's all." It's sobering to note that we all have access to those kinds of transcripts now.

We may soon live in a world wherein parents have access to godlike powers of omniscience. This is the theme of the second episode of the fourth season of *Black Mirror*: "Arkangel" (directed by Jodie Foster). The episode is set in a future wherein helicopter parents can have chips implanted in their children's heads which track their movements and control what they see (by pixelating anything violent, sexual, or potentially upsetting). Among other things, the "Arkangel" technology allows parents to see whatever their kid is seeing at any given moment on something that looks like an iPad.

This godlike power proves irresistible to a single-mother, Marie, when her teenage daughter, Sara, is late coming home one night. She turns on the device just in time to watch her daughter having sex with her boyfriend for the first time. As you might expect, Marie meddles in her daughter's life to a scandalous extent. Sara eventually figures out that her mother is spying on her. The power of the Arkangel technology ultimately destroys Marie's relationship with her daughter. The episode ends with her daughter running away from home. Alas, the dystopian parable's message is clear: omniscient power corrupts relationships.

We need to return to the simple wisdom of Kahlil Gibran's *The Prophet* (1923): "let there be spaces in your togetherness, And let the winds of the heavens dance between you. Love one another but make not a bond of love: Let it rather be a moving sea between the shores of your souls. Fill each other's cup but drink not from one cup. Give one another of your bread but eat not from the same loaf. Sing and dance together and be joyous, but let each one of you be alone." In this brave new world of ours, letting "there be spaces in your togetherness" means respecting the privacy of the people you love.

25.

Romantic Interlude V: Wedding Day Rainbow

"Marriage is a hopeful, generous, infinitely kind gamble taken by two people who don't know yet who they are or who the other might be, binding themselves to a future they cannot conceive of and have carefully omitted to investigate."—Alain de Botton, *The Course of Love* (2018)

After that horrible Flood, there was an olive leaf, and then a beautiful rainbow: pregnant with the promise of redemption and renewal. Which is why we laughed uncontrollably on the hotel shuttle bus, when a rainbow appeared in the sky above the entrance to Grounds for Sculpture, a New Jersey sculpture garden. Because let's face it, Alanis Morissette was wrong. There's nothing ironic about rain on your wedding day. Especially when you're getting married outside at 6:00 p.m., and it's raining cats and dogs at 5:00 p.m. But the deluge subsided just in time, as if by Divine Intervention, and a magical rainbow appeared, a rainbow that seemed to say that the Flood of tears and freak-outs and blow-ups and money and time and effort was all so very worth it. This wedding—made out of the hearts, wallets, and imaginations of faulted human beings—was perfect in every detail: from the bride's dress to the groom's promise: to grab his wife's ass, each and every day, so long as we both shall live.

When you meet your soulmate, she's not your soulmate; when you meet the one, he's not the one, he's one of the ones. But if you build a life together, and stick together through thick and thin, she will become your soulmate, he will become the one.

Conclusion: Promises, Promises

"To breed an animal that is entitled to make promises—surely that is the essence of the paradoxical task nature has set itself where human beings are concerned? Isn't that the real problem of human beings?"—Friedrich Nietzsche, *On the Genealogy of Morality* (1887)

It's hard to be an exceptionally terrible person in Dostoevsky's world, but Marmeladov pulls it off in *Crime and Punishment* (1866). What makes him especially loathsome is his self-awareness. He's a disreputable drunk and he knows it. Indeed, he seems to delight in confessing his sins, at length, to complete strangers. He tells Raskolnikov that his teenage daughter, Sonya, has been forced to become a prostitute to support the family because he squanders all of his pay on vice. He feels bad about this but persists in his dissolute ways regardless.

Marmeladov is an insightful guy who doesn't want for self-knowledge. But since he's utterly devoid of willpower, he can't seem to translate any of these insights and feelings into meaningful change. The gap that most of us experience between What-We-Do and What-We-Intend-To-Do has become an unbridgeable gulf in men like Marmeladov. He's utterly incapable of keeping promises. He's a slave to whim. And yet the libertine calls *this* freedom!

Promises aren't made to be broken; they're made because they *can* be broken. You don't have to promise to eat next year. And I don't have to promise you that the sun will come up tomorrow. Those things will take care of themselves. We promise to do things that won't take care of themselves. We promise because we know things might not work out. We promise to do something because we know we might not feel like doing it in the future. In so doing, we limit our own freedom to act on whim. But the willpower harnessed by this process endows us with an awesome godlike power, a freedom over fate and fortune, which has intoxicated the human mind at least as far back as Abraham.

Romanticism has taught us to revere the freedom of children: the freedom to be spontaneous, to live in the moment, to do what you feel. But I do not revere the freedom of children. Nor do I miss it. Is there a greater slavery than slavery to whim? To momentary fancy? Romanticism has taught us to revere the mighty river of being. But look around you! Look at the world of wonders around us! We've dammed up the river of being, like beavers, and harnessed its power. And it's made us into what we are: glorious, strange, confused, beautiful question marks. What fascinating creatures we are: bare feet on the cool morning earth, heads in the clouds of distant stars. All these dreams of ours, they keep coming true.

About the Author

John Faithful Hamer is a balding middle-aged know-it-all who drinks too much and self-publishes books on Amazon. He still doesn't know how to swim or drive, and his sense of direction is notoriously unreliable, yet he'd love to tell you where to go. His lack of practical skills is astounding, and his inability to fix things is renowned, yet he'd love to tell you what to do. His mismanagement of time is legendary, as is his inability to remember appointments, yet he fancies himself a philosopher and would love to tell you how to live. He wouldn't survive in a state of nature, of that we can be sure; but he's doing quite well in the big city, which has always been a refuge for the ridiculous, a haven for the helpless, and a friend to the frivolous.

Afterword: Does He Ever Shut Up?

When I was seven-years-old, my uncle Nigel was kind enough to take me to the movies with his two kids (my cousins). Apparently my running commentary was maddening. I talked so much through the movie that my frustrated five-year-old cousin Louis-Nicolas started crying. He turned to his father and said: "Does he ever shut up?" I like to think I've changed. But I doubt it. Because this book is largely a product of me being unable to shut up on Facebook.

Most ancient philosophers wrote little or nothing. They received and transmitted their ideas via the spoken word. Some did this of necessity because they were illiterate. But most did so, like Socrates, because they were profoundly suspicious of the written word. The spirit of philosophy was first and foremost, they thought, a function of speeches not scribbles. It couldn't be captured in chirography, but it could be conjured in conversation—and to some extent, encapsulated in aphorisms. Roman soldiers who could barely read often managed, despite their lack of learning, to commit much of Epictetus's *Enchiridion* to memory. Likewise, many an Epicurean shopkeeper living in, say, 2nd-century Athens, would, though functionally illiterate, memorize most (if not all) of Epicurus's aphorisms.

After centuries of decline, the aphorism is back, largely due to social media. In *The Joyful Wisdom* (1887), Nietzsche rightly observes that "the way people write letters" will always be the true "sign of the times." And how do we write letters today? Where is "the style and spirit" of them made manifest? In the aphoristic nature of the tweet, the rough and ready, martial practicality of the text, and the confessional intimacy of the Facebook status update. There is a kind of savage beauty to the literary culture of Social Media Land that charms me to no end. If this Afterword has a purpose, it is to convey something of that savage beauty. All of these aphorisms were originally social media posts.

1. Telling someone who's heartbroken to get over it is sort of like scratching an itch with a razor-blade.
2. Our ancestors cherry-picked scriptures to make their opinions seem like facts, we cherry-pick studies and science-y sounding facts; they said "It is written," we say "Studies have shown."
3. A friend's true colors are visible only after your friendship ceases to be convenient.
4. When we're in love, the world's a dream and we walk on clouds, like angels; when we're with friends, the world makes sense and we walk the earth barefoot, like gods.
5. Banter is what happens to conversation when it learns how to dance.
6. Telling someone who's losing it to calm down is sort of like putting out a fire with gasoline.
7. The only thing harder than speaking truth to power is speaking truth to friends.
8. If it's popular and it looks easy, it's probably not; if you think you could do better, you're probably wrong.
9. "Be yourself, follow your heart, and do what feels right for you," said the therapist, to her patient, the serial killer.
10. Social change is like the ambulance that never seems to be coming fast enough when you're the one in pain.
11. "You're too good for me" is the sweetest way to say "I don't

like you."

12. Breakup sex is as mind-blowing as it is confusing precisely because it combines the excitement of the one-night stand with the expertise of the long-term relationship.

13. All's *not* fair in love and war.

14. *Hookup Ethics 101:* Sometimes YES means YES and NO means NO. But not always. There are NOs that contain a little YES, and YESes that contain a little NO. If in doubt about the former, take NO for an answer; if in doubt about the latter, wait for the hard YES. NO doesn't always mean NO, but it always means STOP.

15. Nobody falls in love quite like an actor.

16. Porn is erotica with bad lighting and a zoom lens.

17. When guys talk about sports in public, you're impressed by their attention to detail; when they talk about sex, you're depressed by it.

18. What's good for the geese isn't always good for the gander.

19. We look for love but are found by friendship.

20. Real friends save you from your enemies in wartime; in peacetime, they save you from yourself.

21. You know who your friends are on moving day.

22. If you think your friends are all crazy, you need to redefine normal; if you think they're all normal, you don't know them very well.

23. You don't have to respect all of your friends' obsessions, but you do have to respect their lack of interest in some of yours.

24. "It takes many sorts to make a world." Wittgenstein considered this "a very beautiful and kindly saying" and so do I. Arrogant twenty-somethings believe a world filled with people just like them would be Heaven; sensible forty-somethings know it would be Hell.

25. Just as Christmas is more fun when you believe in Santa Claus, falling in love is more fun when you believe in the

one.

26. If you find yourself asking "Is he Mr. Right or Mr. Right Now?", he's Mr. Right Now.

27. Ultimatums are addictive. Concede to an unreasonable demand today, and you'll be forced to do so again tomorrow. So if they try to force you to choose between them and *x*, choose *x*.

28. Real friends, like the real mother in 1 Kings 3:16-28, never ask you to cut the baby in half.

29. Like dancing a duet or making love, friendship can't be done alone.

30. To define "real friend" solely with reference to one type of real friend is to inadvertently undervalue some of the most precious people in your life.

31. codependent relationship, *n.* Meaningful relationship.

32. To lose your mind, spend a month alone; to lose yourself, spend a month without any time alone.

33. Challenging the efficacy of talk therapy in secular circles is like challenging the power of prayer in evangelical ones.

34. Misery loves distraction far more than company.

35. Losing an old friendship is like losing a limb: you learn to live without it, but you never stop feeling its absence.

36. friend price, *n.* Price demanded by someone who doesn't value you.

37. A friend who severs ties because of a minor difference of opinion was never a friend.

38. Like bad breath and an accent, a chip on the shoulder always seems to be something others have.

39. Good friends tell you what they think without expecting you to think it too.

40. Having an answer for everything is the infallible sign of not having an answer for everything.

41. irrational, *adj.* Not convinced by your rationalizations.

42. Ideologues are like terrible poker players who don't realize

that every tenth word that comes out of their mouth is a tell.

43. I've never missed a friend I lost over politics.

44. Just as a net that catches the whole sea isn't much of a net, an argument that explains everything isn't much of an argument.

45. The perfect isn't necessarily the enemy of the good, but it's always the enemy of the lazy.

46. Thinking prefabricated thoughts 24/7 is sort of like moving into a prefabricated suburban home: you get to choose the drapes, what color to paint the walls, but little else.

47. On good days, talking to an ideologue is like talking to an answering machine that answers all questions with one of ten prerecorded responses; on bad days, it's like talking to a doctor who prescribes the same three prescriptions to all of his patients, all day long, regardless of what they say to him.

48. Conservatives wrap themselves in the flag of tradition to cover up their naked lust for power; radicals think they can shed the past like a coat and leave the house naked in the middle of winter.

49. Removing a well-established institution from your society is like having a seemingly superfluous body-part surgically removed.

50. Just as you don't have to outrun the bear, just the other guy, your political proposal doesn't have to be perfect, just better than the other guy's.

51. Intellectuals who traffic in anti-intellectualism are like guys who act woke so they can sleep with progressive women.

52. When confronted with new information, the intellectual's first thought is "Is this true?" The ideologue's first thought is "Is this useful to my side?"

53. woke, *adj.* In agreement with me.

54. Wise generals know when it's time to fall back and give ground; but an ideologue never misses an opportunity to

rush in and defend a weak position.

55. Being ideological erodes your creativity far more than it erodes your humanity.

56. Moderates don't have a monopoly on the virtue of moderation.

57. Like children who sword fight with sticks, ideologues who argue with straw men are utterly unprepared for the real thing.

58. Most critiques of social justice warriors are in fact covert defenses of another vision of social justice.

59. Vegans are veganism's biggest PR problem.

60. At a certain point, you've got to face up to the fact that they're not going to face up to the facts.

61. Those who can make you commit atrocities, can make you believe absurdities.

62. Demonize everyone who *seems* to disagree with you and you'll invariably end up strengthening support for those who *actually* disagree with you.

63. You are an ideologue if most of those who disagree with you blur, in your mind, into a single broad category.

64. Fundamentalism is ethics for the dimwitted and morally infantile. It's *Morality for Dummies*.

65. Scratch a critic of social justice warriors and a status quo warrior bleeds.

66. "All this hyperbole is killing us," said the self-described moderate, without a hint of irony.

67. The road to Hell is only paved with good intentions in retrospect. At the time, you think you're on the revolutionary road to Heaven. And there's but one thing which suggests that something might be awry: the road's lined with human roadkill.

68. Just as there are viruses that spare the weak and kill the strong, there are ideas that spare the simple and ruin the clever.

69. *The Principle of Uncharity:* Words mean whatever we mean them to mean when we're using them, but they mean whatever we feel like they mean when you're using them.

70. Hiding within many a zealot is a frightened outsider desperately trying to pass a loyalty test.

71. The Terror snowballs into an avalanche because most figure its initial victims had it coming.

72. You are an ideologue or a coward if there's one group of friends you never piss off.

73. The knock-knock joke falls apart if you refuse to say "Who's there?"

74. Democracy, in practice, isn't rule by the majority; it's rule by highly motivated minorities.

75. If we have to change everything before we can change anything we will change nothing.

76. The arc of the moral universe only bends toward justice when we bend it.

77. Sometimes it is what it is because you keep saying *it is what it is.*

78. If you can't get your people to show up, your people might as well not exist.

79. Just as being politically incorrect is in certain circles a kind of political correctness, accusing others of virtue signaling is in certain circles a kind of virtue signaling.

80. The heroic history of activism is filled with images of triumphant dragon-slayers standing over the carcasses of dragons who died of old age.

81. Refusing to choose the lesser of two evils is often evil.

82. A system that's not working well for you isn't necessarily a system that's not working well.

83. Ugly situations make all but the saints among us ugly, and most of us are not saints. So if you wish to alleviate suffering, stop expecting us to be saints and start fighting ugly situations.

84. A group that includes too many probably has no soul; a group that excludes too many probably has no power.

85. To keep tabs on a radical political group, send a spy; to disrupt them, send an agent provocateur; to destroy them, send no one but lead them to believe they've been infiltrated.

86. Police your crooks and crazies or be defined by them.

87. If something embarrassing becomes public, when they've got dirt on everybody, the first question to ask is "Who benefits?" not "Is this true?"

88. We never seem to reach the end that justified the means.

89. Some people encourage us by encouraging us, others do so by attacking us.

90. At their best, political hacks watch the news the way hungry hyenas watch the watering hole; at their worst, they surf the net looking for fresh tragedy the way vultures fly around looking for fresh roadkill.

91. Nobody speaks truth to power quite like the powerful.

92. If being wrong teaches you how to be humble and admit error graciously, being thought wrong teaches you how to be brave and stand your ground courageously.

93. When you call out injustice, are you motivated by love of the underprivileged or hatred of the privileged? Do you want to help the Have-Nots or hurt the Haves? When you find an inconsistency between high and low, do you try to raise the low or bring down the high?

94. Like machiavellian bureaucrats who require that all would-be complainants wait in line for hours and fill out ridiculously long forms, those who maintain that you have to walk your talk to talk are usually just trying to shut you up.

95. If the gulf between your walk and your talk is a yawning grand canyon, you should probably shut up.

96. down-to-earth, *adj.* As unexceptional as me; devoid of

excellence; that which does not make me feel inadequate or insecure.

97. If the Devil's greatest trick was to convince the world he doesn't exist, the wealthy populist's greatest trick is to convince Joe Average and Regular Rhonda that he's down-to-earth.

98. To be able to charm enemies and win over critics without losing friends: this is the hallmark of political genius.

99. Our political system ensures that everybody's to some extent dissatisfied and nobody gets everything they want—and that's probably the sweetest thing you can say about it.

100. Like the Mona Lisa or Chartres Cathedral, justice is something we create; we don't find it in the world, we bring it to the world.

101. If they're going to criticize you regardless of what you say or do, their criticism probably isn't worth much.

102. With great power comes great plausible deniability.

103. *Golden Rule of Social Media Land:* Thou shalt be, at minimum, nice or interesting; to be both is delightful but rare; to be neither is unforgivable.

104. Twitter feed, *n.* An ongoing stream of messages that lets you know who all the good people are ganging up on at the moment.

105. People who believe in the efficacy of privacy settings are so quaint and cute. It's like talking to people who still believe in the rhythm method.

106. Duck and cover drills gave the 1950s a false sense of security we get from privacy settings.

107. Fake news spreads because smart people who really ought to know better cynically conclude that the righteous end justifies the mendacious means.

108. sharer's remorse, *n.* The deep sense of regret that washes over you when you realize you've shared something really

stupid on social media.

109. Listening to British journalists argue about the royals is like listening to astrologers squabble about the stars.

110. Watching a couple break up in Social Media Land is like watching two recently bitten characters in a zombie movie argue about who's gonna turn first.

111. Don't air your dirty laundry on social media; bad memories fade, but Facebook's forever.

112. "Look," said the asshole, "I'm not an asshole; but I play one on Twitter."

113. like buzz, *n.* The endorphin rush that follows a well-received social media post.

114. The only thing worse than watching a couple break-up on Facebook, is watching a friend break-up with Facebook on Facebook.

115. Every online discussion with a woker-than-thou ideologue feels like that scene in Monty Python's *Life of Brian* (1979), wherein John Cleese's character tells Brian: "If you want to join the People's Front of Judea, you have to really hate the Romans."

116. personal trainer, *n.* Grown man who posts more half-naked selfies than a teenage girl.

117. Being right doesn't give you the right to be boring, nor does it give you the right to be an asshole. Just as enmity is fully compatible with civility, those who disagree can agree to be witty.

118. Spend too much time in a dog park, leave with smelly shoes; too much time online, fall for fake news.

119. Defriend and block all those who publicly post private correspondence without permission, even if they're on your side. Sooner or later, they'll do it to you.

120. legacy media outlet, *n.* News organization that devotes considerable resources to fact-checking.

121. Good news organizations are not unbiased. They have

articulate, consistent bias for which you can correct.

122. trumping, *v.* Spending an inordinate amount of time on the Internet obsessing over Trump's latest antics.

123. fish pic, *n.* Duck face for dudes.

124. 1893 gave us The Scream, 1904 gave us The Thinker, and 2019 gave us The Texter.

125. You know you're on Instagram when you post about a massacre in a New Zealand mosque and the first comment is from a woman in Montreal who wants you to look at her butt.

126. Beware of all those in whom the urge to punch strangers is strong.

127. What a tangled web we weave when we choose to conceive.

128. Parental patience is overrated. Some of the most obnoxious people I know are assholes precisely because they had saints for mothers.

129. Arguing with a kid is like arguing with an internet troll: they're not listening and you're not thinking.

130. The best way to teach your kids to respect their elders is to respect *your* elders.

131. *Parenting Math:* Taking care of two kids is never twice as hard as taking care of one kid (i.e., $2 \times 1 = 2$). It's either $1 \div 2 = \frac{1}{2}$ or $2^2 = 4$. When they're getting along, it's a dream; when they're not, it's a nightmare.

132. There's a special spot in Purgatory reserved for retailers who put up their Christmas decorations on November 1st and parents who take their kids out trick-or-treating at five.

133. Nobody gives me the creeps more than prim and proper parents with spotless houses and flawless lives; nobody speeds when they've got a body in the trunk.

134. premature ejacorator, *n.* Someone who habitually puts up holiday decorations unseasonably early.

135. *How to Have a Clean House:* Step 1: Have no job. Step 2: Have no life. Step 3: Have no kids. Step 4: Have no pets.

Step 5: Eat out often. Step 6: Clean all day. Step 7: Repeat Step 6 daily.

136. When kids say "I'm bored" they usually mean "entertain me"; when adults say "I'm busy" they usually mean "you're boring."

137. *Divorcing Ethics 101:* Everything you do to hurt your ex, hurts your kids.

138. collateral divorcage, *n.* Harm done to innocent bystanders by the explosive dissolution of a long-term relationship.

139. A normal family is a family you don't know very well.

140. The world doesn't owe you a living, but your tribe does.

141. Homeownership domesticates a man far more than marriage.

142. Highborn patrician Publius Clodius Pulcher unwittingly inaugurated a pernicious political tradition when he reinvented himself as Joe Average to get elected in 59 BCE.

143. Being too nice is rarely a problem for those who claim that their problem is that they're just too nice.

144. Tell the fortunate they deserve it and they'll like you; tell them the unfortunate deserve it and they'll love you.

145. teaching critical thinking, *v.* Teaching students how to think like you.

146. The number of rich people who conceal their privileged origins in 21st-century America is roughly equivalent to the number of noblemen who hid their humble origins in ancien-régime France.

147. Lack of privilege reveals as much as it conceals.

148. privilege laundering, *v.* To hide one's privileged origins by fabricating a history of oppression or stressing the importance of a distant underprivileged ancestor.

149. "Sources say" (Journalish) = "I think" (English)

150. We ask for advice when we're looking for permission.

151. The 16th century sold indulgences, the 21st sells carbon credits.

152. Celebrities are like punks who complain about stranger stares after getting facial tattoos.

153. active listening, *n.* Pretend listening.

154. Gourmet kitchens are the parlors of the 21st century: a fancy room that's rarely used.

155. It's surprisingly easy to love people you don't know and apologize for things you didn't do.

156. "You have nothing to fear but fear itself," said the spider to the fly.

157. empowering, *adj.* Infantilizing.

158. The 20th century said "I just buy *Playboy* for the articles," the 21st says "I just work out because it makes me feel good."

159. Celebrities spend the first half of their lives desperately trying to get noticed by the public; the second half is spent complaining about how often they get noticed in public.

160. Apologizing too often is rarely a problem for those who claim that their problem is that they apologize too often.

161. If the murky bathwater's full of shit, don't pretend it's pristine just because there's a baby in it.

162. Epistemic privilege is the last refuge of a scoundrel.

163. Though rare in free societies, flawless public confessions are rather common in totalitarian ones.

164. People who habitually denigrate money would be far more convincing if they didn't ask you for it so often.

165. rhetorical gerrymandering, *v.* Unilaterally redefining the borders of a word's meaning to win an argument.

166. Humans are status-seeking creatures and unethical people cut corners. So if a culture celebrates heroes, unethical status-seekers are going to fake histories of heroism; if it celebrates victims, they'll fake histories of victimization.

167. We love hearing the unvarnished truth for a change, so long as it's not about anything or anyone we love.

168. The only thing most people want to hear less than a lie is the truth.

169. We prefer fantasy to reality because reality is fantastic; it's just not fantastic in the ways we want it to be.

170. The fact that the truth is stranger than fiction is precisely why we prefer fiction.

171. *Documentary Filmmaker's Credo:* And ye shall know the truth, and the truth shall make you miserable.

172. The *veritas* in the *vino* isn't necessarily the truth, but at least it's truthful.

173. If you can't be wrong you probably are.

174. A nerd is someone who's publicly acknowledged that something you deem pointless brings them pure and unadulterated joy.

175. elites, *n.* Smart people who disagree with me.

176. Early to bed, early to rise, makes a man healthy, wealthy, and dull as fuck.

177. vice signaling, *v.* Flaunting your faults to put people at ease and build trust.

178. The tree of civility must be refreshed from time to time with the blood of outspoken scolds and inconsiderate douche-bags.

179. Everyone you love is going to die. You're going to die. None of this ends well.

180. "My problem," said the self-absorbed narcissist at the yoga retreat, "is that I'm just too giving. I really need to learn how to be a little more selfish. How to set aside a little more, you know, me time."

181. narcissitter, *n.* Single person who manages to strategically occupy an entire four-top table at a coffee shop.

182. The 1960s gave us "All you need is love," the 2010s gave us "I'mma worry 'bout me, give a fuck about you."

183. If he's the hero in all of his stories, beware; if he's the victim in all of them, run!

184. narcissist, *n.* Someone who doesn't love you as much as you love you.

185. Wisdom is dawning in a person when they begin to realize that what's good or bad for them isn't necessarily good or bad.

186. The exceptionally selfish and the exceptionally ideological have at least one thing in common: they tend to believe that, deep down, we're all like them. Those who deny it are either lying or in denial. This is a failure of the imagination.

187. philosopher, *n.* A person who fails to see that the unexamined life is in fact well worth living.

188. sociologist, *n.* A person who believes everybody's blinded by social forces, everybody but sociologists.

189. historian, *n.* Hunter who prefers dead prey.

190. journalist, *n.* Someone who brags about how often he's lied (to get information out of people) and then expects you to trust him.

191. We respect historians more than sociologists because the people historians write about can't talk back.

192. If you can't remember the source, it probably doesn't exist.

193. The greater the insecurity, the longer the footnotes; the thicker the jargon, the thinner the thought.

194. Safe spaces usually aren't safe.

195. Aquinas says the argument from authority is the weakest kind of argument. Or was it Aristotle?

196. Just as macho guys hate to look weak, professional victims hate to look strong.

197. The story that's obviously true is often the one you need to fact-check the most.

198. It's hard to detect bullshit when your entire field is already knee-deep in it.

199. We read sociology to realize how utterly typical our seemingly atypical lives are.

200. Tolerance isn't tolerance unless it hurts. We tolerate the

heat. We tolerate the cold.

201. Be careful lest, in casting out your inconsistencies, you cast out the best thing that is in you.

202. The open society isn't a safe space, it's a tolerant space.

203. Much of what passes for tolerance is in fact glorified indifference.

204. It's easy to be open-minded about things you don't care about.

205. Tolerance without reasonable limits is like walking around with a "KICK ME" sign you put on your own back.

206. If human and chimp DNA is 98.8% the same, sameness is probably overrated.

207. I loved John Lennon's "Imagine" for a few decades until I took it seriously for a few minutes.

208. You can't bridge difference in any meaningful way until you acknowledge that it exists.

209. Cultivate your taste without becoming a prisoner of it; you can know and appreciate the best without needing it.

210. The Epicurean princess is sensitive enough to know the pea is there, but too Stoic to care.

211. We must be ruined for the real before we can be sold on the ideal.

212. The easygoing forget resentments almost as readily as they forget commitments.

213. If you have to ask how much it costs, you don't need it.

214. Misunderstood geniuses are rare; misunderstood mediocrities who fancy themselves geniuses are not.

215. Never mistake symmetry for balance, sweetness for stupidity, or enthusiasm for gullibility.

216. An Epicurean is person who values routine pleasures and routinely questions the value of novel ones.

217. Just as men never shut up about how women have all the real power in places where women have no real power, the rich prate on and on about the happy poor in places where

the poor are miserable.

218. A mind that has lost the ability to forget is like a body in the midst of acute renal failure.

219. Time doesn't fly when you're having fun, it flies when you're old; when you're having fun, time stops.

220. Writers come in two types: Snow Whites who sit around waiting for their prince to come, and James Joyces who put themselves out there again and again and again.

221. pundit, n. A writer who is always ready to respond to breaking news with a thoughtful opinion piece he wrote years ago.

222. When unsuccessful writers review the works of commercially successful writers, they invariably talk about how easy it is to write a commercially successful book.

223. Listening to writers complain about their inability to attract readers is like listening to flowers complain about their inability to attract bees.

224. The pen is only mightier than the sword if you've got a lot of Instagram followers.

225. If you haven't lived enough, you don't have anything to say; if you haven't read enough, you don't know how to say it.

226. God save us from the literal-minded! They're killing us!

227. Most writers fail to realize that the gatekeepers they spend so much time sucking up to are holding the keys to bankrupt, depopulated kingdoms.

228. Publishing has gone from swords to guns and yet most writers still prance around like wannabe knights.

229. Don't judge a book by its cover, unless there's a PhD after the author's name.

230. We want a diagnosis from the expert far more than a cure.

231. If I see *The Secret* (1994) on someone's shelf, someone I've recently met and like, my heart sinks and I cry inside for a minute or two. But if I see it on the shelf of someone I've recently met and don't like, I nod knowingly to myself,

because everything makes sense now.

232. Finishing a great novel is like watching a dying star devour a blue-green planet that has come to feel like home.

233. To be a nonfiction bestseller, one must perfect the art of landing on an inhabited continent of thought and declaring it discovered.

234. Words like "racist" and "violence" are like plastic bags: you can stretch them a bit, but they break and become useless if you put too much stuff in them.

235. The phrase "to make a long story short" is usually uttered at the beginning of the second half of the long version of a short story.

236. If a language is a dialect with an army, good grammar is what language sounds like when power speaks.

237. Every tired old cliché was once a beautiful young aphorism.

238. Demanding that linguistic conventions stay the same is like telling your ten-year-old to stop growing up.

239. Correcting grammar is like building a sandcastle when the tide's coming in. It should be done with a playful seriousness. Ain't no reason to get all moralistic 'bout it.

240. Just as the Ottomans castrated their servants to render them reliable servants of their power, modern professionals castrate the language they use to render it a reliable servant of their power.

241. The sterility of professional jargon isn't a bug, it's a feature.

242. Free speech is decried more often than not by those who aren't particularly good at speech.

243. When you deprive language of its freedom to be somewhat slippery, squishy, and imprecise, you deprive it, as well, of its talismanic power to illuminate the world around us.

244. proper channels, n. Channels nobody listens to.

245. Even in the worst tyrannies, speech is free where nobody's listening.

246. stonewalling, v. Refusing to talk to someone who's not

listening.

247. Real men dont stop & ax for directshuns from a dickshunary.

248. Sometimes language changes to reflect a newfound understanding of reality; sometimes it changes to reflect a newfound discomfort with reality.

249. Euphemisms are the fig leaves we sew together when we feel naked in the presence of truth.

250. The right to free speech doesn't come with a concomitant right to be taken seriously.

251. Free speech needs to be for everyone, including those who don't deserve it, for the same reason that Universal Basic Income needs to be for everyone, including those who don't need it.

252. The road to effective communication is paved with silly analogies and irresponsible metaphors.

253. Looking for four-leaf clovers teaches you how to avoid false patterns and detect exceptions; finding them teaches you that the uncommon is actually quite common.

254. Looking for salamanders teaches you how to slow down and be patient; finding them teaches you that beauty is often to be found among the little things in life.

255. Finding a salamander under a log in the woods is like catching a monk curled up in prayer.

256. Overcoming the natural: could anything be more natural for a human being?

257. Listening to someone who lives in the 21st-century West talk about what's natural is sort of like listening to Rick James tell someone to ease off on the coke in Studio 54.

258. If getting cancer at 40 proves that life isn't fair, getting zits at 14 proves that it's malicious too.

259. *Dinosaur Wisdom:* Nothing is too big to fail; specialization leads to fragility; generalists are more likely to survive black swan events—as are smaller creatures, like salamanders,

with slow metabolisms and low-cal overhead costs.

260. If the demagogue says what everybody wants to hear, and the comedian says what nobody wants to say, the prophet says what nobody wants to hear.

261. A prophet is honored everywhere except in his own hometown—if it's an insecure backwater like Nazareth; self-confident cities have no trouble honoring their own.

262. "Watch out for that web," said the butterfly to the bee. "Quit being so paranoid," said the spider with a smile.

263. Prophets prophesy to prevent the prophecy, not to predict it.

264. If you can see the future, you don't talk about it, you bet on it.

265. *Popular Joke:* A prophet, a comedian, and a demagogue walk into a bar. The prophet tells everyone to beware of the demagogue but nobody listens. The comedian makes fun of the prophet and everyone laughs. The demagogue tells everyone drinks are on him, then he skips out on the bill.

266. Prophets are often right about the prophecy but wrong about the timing.

267. What doesn't kill you increases your deductible.

268. Obsession is like a fast-moving river: if you can't get out of it, go with the flow; sooner or later, even the mightiest rivers empty out into calmer waters.

269. Commercial, *adj.* Successful.

270. labor of love, *n.* Unprofitable project.

271. surreal, *adj.* Not like the movies.

272. People who tend to find a lot of beauty in the world tend to spend a lot of time looking for it.

273. Willingness to get wet is an excellent indicator of a person's true age.

274. Squirrels are just rats with excellent PR.

275. beautiful soul, *n.* A pathologically irresponsible person who smiles a lot.

276. If you ain't feelin' the kiss, it wasn't made for your lips. If you ain't feelin' the beat, it wasn't made for your hips. If the song sounds like noise, the angels aren't singing it for you.

277. If the sight of the blue skies fills you with joy, if a blade of grass springing up in the fields has power to move you, if the simple things of nature have a message that you understand, rejoice, for your meds are working.

278. Anger is the most self-justifying of the emotions; it's also the most intoxicating.

279. Yelling is a language everybody can speak but nobody understands.

280. Like wing mirrors on cars, atrocity porn should come with a warning: *Atrocities in this Disturbing Image May Not Warrant Military Intervention.*

281. Although there are plenty of good reasons to be pissed off, being perpetually pissed off doesn't necessarily make you a good person.

282. If the death of one is a tragedy, and the death of a million is a statistic, the death of a few dozen is BREAKING NEWS!

283. Everything translated into Yelling is lost in translation.

284. Grief is best articulated by those who view it from the middle distance. If you're too far away, you probably don't know what you're talking about. If you're too close, you're probably too stunned to speak.

285. As the Harry Potter series makes clear, sometimes the only way to deal with something horrific is to make fun of it.

286. In Hell, you're strapped to an uncomfortable couch covered in cat hair and forced to eat vegan baked goods whilst listening to wind chimes and watching renovation shows. Forever.

287. The opposite of love isn't hate, it's renovation shows.

288. Living paycheck-to-paycheck is like getting stalked by a hungry lion that never quite catches you, and never goes away. And debt's the leg weights that render you fast

enough to jog but too slow to run.

289. Microsoft Office killed far more jobs than NAFTA.

290. Bad trade deals will never be as disruptive as good software.

291. You can't bring back jobs that didn't go anywhere.

292. There's no "i" in team, but there's a couple in idiot.

293. If business doesn't exist to employ people, the people's government shouldn't exist to employ business.

294. Though meetings rarely, if ever, make your day, they can ruin it with some regularity.

295. To halve the amount of email you receive, check your email half as often.

296. The 12th century believed in alchemy, the 21st believes jobs lost due to automation are magically replaced.

297. Deal with bills promptly and you get fewer of them; deal with emails promptly and you get more of them.

298. How is it that we hear the loudest yelps for meritocracy among people who got their jobs through connections?

299. Even Solomon ceases to be Solomon when he's forced to adjudicate too many cases a day.

300. If time flies when you're having fun, joy dies when measuring's won.

301. If Santa was like the free market, he'd deliver twice as many gifts but skip half the houses.

302. Branding used to be something done to slaves and livestock by force; today, we do it to ourselves.

303. 80% of success is showing up and getting lucky.

304. HR loves diversity training and anti-bullying campaigns for the same reasons law enforcement loves the War on Drugs and the War on Terror.

305. No matter where you are, or what you're doing, if you keep checking the time, you're at work.

306. stakeholder, n. A subject who used to be a citizen.

307. Nothing says "I don't want an office job" quite like facial tattoos.

308. Nothing beats the unwinnable war if you're trying to justify your budget.

309. Never underestimate how little your big problem matters to a bureaucrat.

310. A computer used to be a person who believed a machine couldn't possibly do his job.

311. If Hell exists, and Dante described it accurately, I suspect that there will be a special place in its vestibule reserved for craven administrators who did nothing about known bad apples.

312. The market is like a little kid with a superpower. He's a miraculous multiplier. But he's also kinda messy. And he doesn't share especially well. That's why we need to have some adults in the room: grownups who encourage him to play nice and share his toys.

313. Trying to make capitalism work in a place that lacks the requisite culture and values is like trying to build an igloo in Tahiti.

314. The magic of the market is largely a function of the magic of culture.

315. Asking a bureaucrat for help is like asking an acquaintance to help you move. They don't feel obliged to help you—but they might, regardless, if you're sufficiently charming, and they've got nothing else they'd rather do.

316. Reasonable conversations are undermined, not by those who compare apples and oranges, but by those who compare apples and hand-grenades.

317. unreasonable, *adj.* Not convinced by your reasons.

318. Open-minded people never fail to provide you with at least three different ways to agree with them.

319. Thinking that a better version of the same argument will get through to someone who's momentarily blinded by fear or rage is like thinking that a louder version of the same question will get through to someone who doesn't speak

English.

320. The major obstacle on the road to wisdom isn't stupidity, lack of intelligence, or ignorance, but rather an unwillingness to question that which we love and care about.

321. At some point, the evidence becomes impossible to deny, and you're forced to cancel your subscription to the Flat Earth Society.

322. The best persuaders look up and point; the worst point out why you really ought to look up.

323. If the rules don't apply to everybody they don't apply to anybody.

324. A reputation for being correct is good, but a reputation for self-correction is better. The first is fragile, the second is not.

325. In the beginning was a middle, an anxious middle, who dreamed of a world without beginnings and endings. What is the longing for eternity, if not the longing of a middle, to remain a middle, forever?

326. It's easy to act like lions are more or less harmless when you've grown up with nothing but a toothless old lion in a cage.

327. Religion shapes how you think and believe far more than what you think and believe. That's why getting rid of the idea of Heaven doesn't necessarily rid us of the longing for a painless paradise; why getting rid of the idea of Redemption doesn't necessarily rid us of the longing for an escape from History and Consequence; and why getting rid of The Savior doesn't necessarily rid us of the longing for salvation.

328. Luthecostal, n. A polite Protestant who speaks in but one tongue.

329. The Bible contradicts evolution the way the Icarus story contradicts aerodynamics.

330. I seem to have been predestined to not believe in predestination.

331. woo woo, *n*. Other people's religion.

332. When you call someone a hypocrite, are you trying to get them to walk their talk? Or are you merely trying to get them to stop talking about something that's making you uncomfortable? Are you virtue's friend or vice's apologist? God's advocate? Or the Devil's?

333. If God's a writer and Dante was right, plagiarists will end up in the outer ring of the Seventh Circle of Hell, where they'll be immersed in Phlegethon, a river of boiling blood, to a level commensurate with their sins.

334. Nietzsche was wrong, God's not dead. He's just binge-watching Netflix.

335. Even in a totalitarian theocracy like Gilead, the oppressed are allowed to beat a scapegoat to death from time to time.

336. The success or failure of any big idea depends, to a large extent, upon enthusiastic converts who don't understand it.

337. Catch and cage the mystery and it ceases to sing.

338. The fact-value distinction makes sense in the world of science; but in the messy world of politics, a value somebody is willing to die for is a *de facto* fact, and a fact nobody values scarcely exists.

339. If an eye for an eye leaves the whole world blind, an obsession with hypocrisy leaves morality ill-defined.

340. organized religion, *n*. Religion.

341. One person's sacred cow is another person's filet mignon.

342. If all you've got are thoughts and prayers, keep them to yourself.

343. People who say they regret nothing, and say so truthfully, are either saints, sociopaths, sages, or stupid.

344. If desperate times call for desperate measures, you can't blame the desperate for doing horrible things to survive, but you can praise them for refusing to do so.

345. If you refuse to do horrible things to survive, even when you're desperate, you're a saint; if you're not desperate, and yet you do horrible things just to win, you're a monster.

346. If you'll do anything to win, and you just can't lose, stop playing the game.

347. Resisting the temptation to do evil is easy when you lack courage and a Ring of Gyges.

348. Curiosity dispels fear at least as often as courage.

349. Thinking someone virtuous merely because they've been victimized in some way is like thinking someone virtuous merely because they've got blue eyes.

350. Our lives should be defined, not by what the world has done to us, but by what we've done in the world.

351. Your ethics are defined primarily, not by what you do, but by what you simply wouldn't do.

352. *The Opposite of Networker*: Someone who's habitually nice to people who won't be useful to him in the future.

353. Learn from your mistakes, don't wallow in them.

354. "We're all human" is the sugar-free gum of human identities: tasty for a second or two but utterly devoid of nutritional value.

355. *Podcasting Ethics 101*: If you spend most of your time trying to sound smart, you're doing it wrong. If you spend any of your time trying to make your guest sound stupid, you're wasting everybody's time. Your primary objectives are to have fun and make your guest sound smart. Since your guests are fascinating people, making them sound smart should be easy: just read up on what they know and play to their strengths, not your own.

356. Any explanation of moral outrage that dismisses all moral outrage as disingenuous bullshit is disingenuous bullshit.

357. An otherwise bright person who doesn't know much about history is like a painter who's forever forced to paint the present with the same five colors; the erudite, with an

extensive knowledge of history, is like a painter with an extensive palette of colors to choose from.

358. The main problem with the past is that it happened.

359. Knowing your history doesn't guarantee you'll get it right all the time, but it does guarantee you'll refrain from comparing everything to Hitler.

360. Even a mushroom cloud can be beautiful from a safe distance.

361. The boy leaped to his feet and sang out as loudly as he could, "Hitler! Hitler!" But the villagers thought he was trying to fool them again, and so they didn't come.

362. To maximize your love of an old institution, minimize your research into its history.

363. old school, *adj.* Popular when you were hot.

364. Win the war and the historians will tell you why your victory was inevitable; lose it and they'll do likewise.

365. Getting a cobra to deal with your rat problem might solve your rat problem; but now you're living with a cobra.

366. revolution hawk, *n.* Activist who advocates revolutionary violence without knowing anything about revolution or violence.

367. If you're being habitually ignored, setting your hair on fire might get you the attention you're looking for; but now your hair's on fire.

368. The problem with pathetic pleas is that they repulse all but the best whilst attracting some of the worst.

369. Movements, organizations, and institutions that prize loyalty above all else are destined for moral disaster; those that act like loyalty doesn't matter have no future.

370. Strive to be liked by all and you're sure to be loved by none.

371. Breaking something that works in practice simply because it doesn't make sense in theory is the height of insanity, and yet we do it all the time.

372. Revolutionary violence is at times necessary but always

tragic; it's romanticized only by fools, sociopaths, and those who've never experienced revolutionary violence.

373. "I don't get it so it must be stupid," said the philistine. "I don't get it so it must be brilliant," said the highbrow. "I don't get it," said the sage.

374. Just as flowers don't demand the attention of bees, the Sirens didn't shipwreck sailors with reprimands.

375. Being constantly contradicted makes you crazy; being rarely contradicted makes you stupid.

376. Like parasites, vices only kill you accidentally.

377. We don't domesticate plants and animals, they domesticate us.

378. First-world farmers get migrant laborers to do all of the backbreaking work; middle-class gardeners do it for free.

379. High-school dropouts work weekends because they have to; middle-class gardeners do it for free.

380. You have no idea how much free time you're forfeiting when you plant a garden or bring home a puppy.

381. We rearrange the furniture on the Titanic when we don't know how to stop it from sinking.

382. Doing nothing can be exhausting and saving money can be expensive.

383. People who say they don't care about their reputation are like carefree twenty-somethings who say they don't care about their health.

384. The chickens who killed the goose that laid the golden eggs clucked and clicked with glee—until the gold ran out.

385. If you habitually go out cruising for a bruising, the guy who finally gives it to you is guilty of assault; but you're also guilty of being an idiot.

386. Nobody likes the voice of prudence because it presupposes that the world isn't as it ought to be.

387. If you think most of the people you meet are idiots, you might be a genius, but you're probably just an asshole.

388. If you don't have anything nice to say, say it in the Comments Section.

389. Although misandry and misogyny are equally evil in theory, their real world consequences are anything but equal: woman-hating men murder women with some regularity, whilst man-hating women are just annoying dinner party guests.

390. Heaven has no rage like self-love to misogyny turned, nor hell a fury like an entitled little asshole scorned.

391. People are remarkably generous with unsolicited advice.

392. "Look," said the asshole, "I'm not an asshole, I just like to tell it like it is."

393. white knight, n. Decent human being who refuses to participate in the bystander effect.

394. The same sort of sleazy guys who became artists a century ago are becoming yoga teachers today. We've gone from "Wanna come upstairs and see my etchings?" to "Wanna come upstairs and see my stretchings?"

395. Saying "Watch out!" when they're heading for a brick wall is an act of kindness; saying "I told you so!" after they've hit it is an act of pettiness.

396. Wind chimes desecrate wind the way elevator music desecrates music.

397. Offensive people tell you to stop being so defensive for the same reason that schoolyard bullies tell you to move your hands out of the way so they can punch you in the face.

398. Our generosity with other people's money is surpassed only by our generosity with other people's time.

399. It takes a village of cheer-leading sycophants and cowardly bystanders to raise an asshole.

400. Familiarity breeds contempt only in the contemptible.

401. We call someone inconsistent when we lack the courage to call them wrong.

402. First they conclude that the truth is always ugly, then they

conclude that everything ugly is true.

403. The faux-feminism popular among wealthy white women allows them to throw their male relatives under the bus whilst sneaking out the back door of Privilege Mansion before the woke bombs hit.

404. Smug is contempt with its fly down.

405. The paradox of World Cup soccer is that the women play like men and the men play like girls.

406. Though both can be bad, true believers are considerably more dangerous than cynics. At their worst, true believers kill you. At their worst, cynics merely stay home and do nothing to prevent the true believers from killing you.

407. Civilization is a beautiful island of order that emerges from time to time, like Atlantis, out of a sea of chaos.

408. The sensitivities of children are inherited, those of civilized adults are cultivated.

409. Manly men used to fight bears and slay dragons; today, they fight bathroom etiquette and spray seats. How far the mighty have fallen.

410. Blessèd are they that do put the toilet seat down: for they shall be called civilized men and housebroken humans.

411. Blessèd are they which do refill the ice-cube tray: for they shall inherit domestic felicity.

412. Blessèd are they who give out candy on Halloween: for they shall be called good neighbors.

413. Accursèd be they who turn off their lights and pretend they're not home on Halloween night: they shall be called cheapskates and bad neighbors.

414. Immigrant communities aren't representative because the representative tend to stay put; it's usually the best and worst who move.

415. Meditating on the meaning of entropy can make a conservative out of any radical. Order is fragile. And the barbarians never really leave the gates.

416. Survivalists who live off the grid and rail against the government are like imaginative children who pretend that they're self-sufficient grownups whilst sitting in a tree house, in mommy and daddy's backyard.

417. "Give them an inch and they'll take a mile" makes sense only if you're dealing with a relentless asshole. If you're dealing with a normal person, being an uncompromising prick invariably backfires. Refuse to give them an inch and you're sure to lose the mile.

418. Wisdom begins with the realization that some things are in fact above your pay-grade.

419. Unless you were probed by a fish-faced alien last night, your problems are probably pretty generic; but that doesn't make them any less problematic.

420. Putting your problems into perspective works well when you're a fly on the wall, not when you're a fly in the web.

421. Sometimes silence is deafening, and sometimes it's the right thing to say, but silence is never silent.

422. wisdom, n. The ability to follow your own advice.

423. If dandelions remind us that beautiful things don't have to be rare, rust reminds us that even our most durable handiwork is as mortal as we are.

424. Our ancestors needed to be reminded that the great in their midst were mere mortals; we need to be reminded that mere mortals can be great.

Other Books by Author

From Here: A Love Letter to Montréal
Welcome to Likeville: Being a Philosopher in Social Media Land

Credits

cover art: Indigo Hamer

Manufactured by Amazon.ca
Bolton, ON

11072199R00087